Tell Me Who I Am

HEATHER ROGERS

HEATHER ROGERS

Copyright © 2012 Heather Rogers

All rights reserved.

ISBN: **978-1975936150**
ISBN-13: **1975936159**

THE HOLY BIBLE, NEW INTERNATIONAL VERSION®, NIV® Copyright © 1973, 1978, 1984, 2011 by Biblica, Inc.® Used by permission. All rights reserved worldwide.

Scripture taken from *The Message*. Copyright © 1993, 1994, 1995, 1996, 2000, 2001, 2002. Used by permission of NavPress Publishing Group.

Scripture quotations are from The ESV® Bible (The Holy Bible, English Standard Version®), copyright © 2001 by Crossway, a publishing ministry of Good News Publishers. Used by permission. All rights reserved.

Scripture taken from the New King James Version®. Copyright © 1982 by Thomas Nelson. Used by permission. All rights reserved.

DEDICATION

To Geoff and Claire, who told me who I am, and had the kindness and gentleness to love me when I hadn't quite got there yet.

To Ru and Jon, Sherryl and Mark, my cheerleaders, who remind me who I am in the moments that I forget.

To Leni, Mabel and Vera; may you always know that you are worth more than gold to Jesus, and to me.

	I Am, Because He Is (Introduction)	8
1	I Am Not	15
2	I Am Good	33
3	I Am Loved	49
4	I Am Attractive	64
5	I Am Strong	75
6	I Am Capable	87
7	I Am Needed	102
8	I Am Kind	115
9	I Am Possible	123
10	I Am a Dreamer: Elaine Grant	135

Things move. Things shift and squirm, and tumble and fall.

They don't work out, they can't find their feet; the things we hope for might not happen at all;

"Sorry love, I just can't make it tonight

I wish I could…" or maybe, this just doesn't feel right.

Maybe I'm saying: "you're just not good enough"

    Too big;

        too small;

           too clever;

but all you're looking for is someone to tell you that **You. Are. Enough.**

    You are worth something. You are beautiful.

So you put on a face, day in, day out:

a face that says "I can do anything".

    A face that is strong, independent; or maybe just a loud mouth.

Nobody can see you, because you don't let them;

no, what they see is just a perception.

They fill in the gaps, make their own person,

    leaving who *you* are up to interpretation.

But there is one who sees through –

who sees through to the you that you are supposed to be.

He's the one that wanted you so much that He made you;

    moulded out of skin and bones,

        hopes and dreams,

           and so beautiful.

He gave you your laugh, your smile –

and maybe He hasn't seen it in a while, but His heart breaks with yours.

    He cries when you cry,

        laughs with your joy;

            sees the heartbreak that you felt over some boy

            who couldn't see you the way that He does.

But I pray that the joy of the Lord will be your strength.

That doesn't mean fake a smile – be OK for a while –

    it means that delight in God is your refuge;

it's your hiding place,

    it's where you go instead of putting on a face,

        a smile, some make-up; just stop,

            and take a moment to look up.

Look up at the Father, your saviour, your friend –

because of Him, this isn't the end.

This doesn't end with us feeling not enough;

    instead, it's Him feeling chuffed: so proud of all that He has done

    that He looks down and says **"I want that kid"**.

And He doesn't move, He doesn't change –

    no, this God is the beginning and the end.

The things we hope for, they're coming, while we're constantly transforming into the person that we are designed to be.

Look up – and see the one smiling down on you.

    Delight in Him; because He delights in you, too.

TELL ME WHO I AM

INTRODUCTION
I AM, BECAUSE HE IS

This is a book about you. It's a book about the things that you're not, and the things that you are, the things that you hate and the things that you love, the things that you've done and the things that you will do. It's about the things that you think you can't do, and the things that you can do, and the things that you would love to do if you had the chance. It's a book about the gold that is inside of you, and the things that other people see in you that you cannot see for yourself yet.

But more than that, this is a book about God: an unshakeable, immovable, unbelievably big God, with a love for you bigger than you could possibly imagine. This is about the God of all creation, who with the same heart that put the stars in the sky, and created the mountaintops, breathed life into you: a life that contains His hope, His joy, His peace, His freedom, if you'll take it.

I have the words to fill this book because some years ago, when I was seventeen, God moved in and showed me a life that is bigger than I could ever imagine without Him. He invited me on an adventure with Him, not trying to work things out on my own, but carving out a journey with my creator. This Jesus-adventure has taken me to Cambridge, it's given me dreams and hopes, and people to care for and love. It has set me up for a life that can make a significant impact on the people around me and He's given me words to speak that change the direction of people's lives for good. I'm on this adventure because a man called Geoff chose to sit sat down next to me and tell me that I am loved; tell me that I'm created, that I'm here for a reason, and that God has a hope and a future for me. Through people like Geoff, Jesus filled my life; He broke into my very comfortable upbringing – middle-class England, good family, good education – a life in which God wasn't necessary because I was doing just fine on my own, thank you very much.

But when Geoff sat down beside me that night, he told me the truth, and introduced me to a life-giving God and a Saviour who walks by our side: whatever life is like without God, life with God is bigger, fuller and has more hope and joy that we can possibly imagine.

My prayer for this book is that I might be your Geoff; may this book be for you a message of a hope and a future, and point you towards Jesus. Maybe you've been a Christian for as long as you can remember, and this book is something that you have picked up as part of your journey with God. That's great – hello! I hope that this book is a great encouragement in your walk with God, a reminder of the love that He has for you, and the potential that you have because of your identity in Him. There are some reflective questions at the end of each chapter that I hope you will find helpful as you stop and take a breath, and spend some time working through these things with Him. This is what, I hope, this book is all about: a little bit of breathing space, a step out of the place that you are in, the people you are around and the things that have happened to you. There's lots of chances for you to take a moment to stop and be honest with yourself about where you are at, what you believe and the way that this is affecting your life and your identity; and my prayer is that this book offers you an opportunity to think differently.

Or maybe you have no idea what I'm talking about; maybe this book was handed to you by a friend, or something you picked up and you're just having a flick through. Maybe you've never thought about faith, or God, and what it would mean to follow Him; maybe you'd rather not. This book is for you, too. I challenge you to give it a read – scribble thoughts in the margins, ask questions, find the things that you agree or don't agree with – and then find someone to chat it through with. Google your local church, find a Christian friend, and let this be the start of the conversation.

Wherever you are coming from, I hope you have a cup of tea in your hand, and a couple of biscuits lined up while you're reading this book. I am not an expert in anything; or a theologian; or an old, wise woman who would sit in a rocking chair while you kneel at my feet and listen to my wisdom. But I'm a friend, I'm a sister, and while I'm still new to this life with God, I've completely fallen in love, and found out who I really am because I get to live in this beautiful relationship with Him.

One thing that I know for certain is that whoever you are, an encounter with the living God brings hope. Let me introduce you to the God that I know. For a long time, when I pictured God in my head, I thought of Morgan Freeman in Bruce Almighty – an elderly guy, sat on a cloud, looking down on me and judging the way that I do things. The God that was in my head saw everything, but that didn't feel good; it felt like I constantly had a scary head teacher figure looking over my shoulder, tutting at my mistakes. And when I tripped, he would pick me up, and would land me back on my feet; but it felt like I had started again, like I had to work my way back up into his good books. Maybe this is like the picture of God that you have in your head – the old man, sat above us, stroking his beard. The guy that you only really need to think about at Christmas and Easter, if that – because the rest of the time, he's just sat up there, minding his own business. He's God; he's got bigger things to think about, right?

But the God that *is* is so different to this Morgan-Freeman-type character that I had in my head. We have a Father in heaven who is love, security, safety, peace and truth; who, in a crazy and confusing world, we can go to to find truth and peace. We can have a direct relationship with the same God who created everything – who put the stars in the sky and who was there before the earth was formed – because we've seen Him reflected in His Son, Jesus, and we have been sent His Holy Spirit as a direct link to this great God. There's so much more about Him all through this book, but this is the perspective that we're coming from: that we were created by this awesome God, who is our heavenly Father, and who sent us a Saviour in Jesus so that we can have a direct relationship with Him.

Life throws all kinds of things at us; but when we walk through the challenging times – when we are trying to work out who we are, when we are going through the valley of the shadow of death – it is not hearing a good sermon or even knowing the right scriptures that will pull us through, but having a direct relationship with the God that they are all about. I hope that, through this book, you will be pointed towards your Father in heaven, who can provide you with all that you need and who loves you more that you could ever imagine. Truth comes from Him, so this book is jammed full of God and His word; not my word, but the word of God – the Bible. That's where we can go to find the truth of who we are. The Bible translation I've normally quoted from is called the New International Version, or NIV, but there are a couple of other translations I've used too!

To be able to really stand on the truth of who we are, we need to be totally assured of who He is – we are only who we are because of who He is. The whole principle of our identity works on an *if, then, so* foundation – *if* God is who He says He is *then* there are certain things that must be true about who we are, and *so* our lives and worlds can be impacted by the truth of who He is. God stands up to His word – He is all that He says He is, and it is shown in His Word. At some point, we must make a decision that the word of God is true: it is that simple, just a decision to believe; and when we do, everything else seems to fall into place. There are always opportunities to say "this doesn't work" and to try to carry on our own way – but faith is putting the truth of God over the uncertainty of our circumstances, and deciding to believe that what He says is true.

I AM

There's lots of things to hear and see in this world, but there are some things that we can only get from God: God is the truth; the Bible is the truth about the truth; theology is the truth about the truth about the truth, and a good sermon or book is the truth about the truth about the truth about the truth. When we are living in relationship with God, we have direct access to the truth of who He thinks we are and who He says He is, and that truth sets us free.

There's a man called Moses in the Bible; and I love this part of the story, because he got to see a glimpse of who God is, and it changed the direction of his life forever. At this point, Moses was having a conversation with God: God had sent him to talk to the people of Israel, and he was having a little bit of a crisis at the request:

> ***Moses said to God, "Suppose I go to the Israelites and say to them, 'The God of your fathers has sent me to you,' and they ask me, 'What is his name?' Then what shall I tell them?" God said to Moses, "I AM who I AM. This is what you are to say to the Israelites: 'I AM has sent me to you.'" (Exodus 3:13-14)***

I AM is the most significant name for God that is found in the Bible, and begins to sum up all that God is for us, and was to Moses in that moment. I AM; because He is self-existent – He exists because of Himself. I AM, because He never changes; He is the same yesterday, today and forever, and He is eternal. I AM, because He is incomprehensible; we cannot know all that there is to know about Him – we can't work Him out and rationalise His existence. I AM, because He is unchangeable in His word and His nature; He is faithful and true to all the He says that He is. I AM, because He is a person; not a force, not a spiritual thing that we can connect with, but a living God who is more of a person than it is possible for you and I to be.

I AM, because He is everything that we need Him to be, and we can look to Him for all things. I AM the provider. I AM the healer. I AM the beginning and the end. I AM the life giver. I AM the joy-bringer. I AM the supplier of peace. He is everything that we need; He is the Source that provides us with all good things. This is His name: it's who He is, it's what He wants to do; He is actively pursuing a relationship with you, and wants to be the I AM to all that you need and hope for. This is faith: knowing that He is the I AM to all that we need, and that He has already achieved all that needed to be done, provided us with all that we need and healed us of every sickness and iniquity.

There's a lot behind our name. Here, God revealed His name to Moses, and Moses could begin to understand who God is. In the Bible, a *name* is more than just a name: it's a character, a personality, a life. So, when we know God's name, we can begin to know who God is, and when we know who God is, we can have an intimate relationship with Him. When we know God, we can recognise God at work in our lives and in our world; we can point others towards Him. It means that our God-knowledge is not just head knowledge, not just facts; but deep, experiential knowledge that changes our hearts.

And because of who God is, we can have freedom and confidence in who we are:

For this reason I kneel before the Father, from whom every family in heaven and on earth derives its name. I pray that out of his glorious riches he may strengthen you with power through his Spirit in your inner being, so that Christ may dwell in your hearts through faith.

(Ephesians 3:14-17)

Strength and boldness do not come from a "fake it until you make it" attitude. Boldness comes from a knowledge of the truth of who you are, and the truth of who God is in you, because Christ dwells in your heart through faith. Your name is His name, because you are in Christ. When two people get married, the wife takes on the name of her husband as a seal of the bond that they have in marriage; and this is what Christ does for us. My being is not found in the earthly things, but in being hidden in Him, and in being a child of God. You have the name of Jesus – this is not just a name that you can borrow when you need it; it has power, and is free for you to use. In living in your true identity, it is not you that is working, but Him that is working through you. And because the love of God is in you, you can comprehend the love of Christ; you can know who He is and have a relationship with Him.

The Old Testament is full of stories of people who were seeking God: this far off, sovereign God, who dwelled in the Holy of Holies, separated from His people by a curtain. His people were under a law that no man could live up to; no man was worthy of standing in the presence of God. But here's the promise that was given to the people through the prophet Malachi, the last book in the Old Testament:

"I will send my messenger, who will prepare the way before me. Then suddenly the Lord you are seeking will come to His temple; the messenger of the covenant, whom you desire, will come" (Malachi 3:1)

The temple was a concept that the people understood, because that was where they sought Him so desperately. They had a promise of God coming to meet them where they had been seeking Him – and from a God who remains the same, and who keeps His promises. He says this:

"So I will come to put you on trial. I will be quick to testify against sorcerers, adulterers and perjurers, against those who defraud labourers of their wages, who oppress the widow and the fatherless, and deprive the foreigners among you of justice, but do not fear me" (Malachi 3:5)

Here, right at the end of the Old Testament, we begin to see the difference between the old relationship that God had with His people, the law, and the relationship that we have because of Jesus: grace. While the Old Testament is full of rules and laws that were put on the people, an impossible standard to live up to, Jesus brings grace, covering our sin. Here, we see the things that really matter to Him: a promise to bring judgement on sorcerers, those that steal wages from labourers, those who oppress widows and orphans, who tread down God's children, those who do not stand up for the foreigners – the refugees! This is the real calling that He has given us, and if we ignore it then we are going against the very nature of God.

And then the beginning of the Gospels tells of the life of Jesus, fulfilling the promise that was given to the people in the Old Testament:

And so John the Baptist appeared in the wilderness, preaching a baptism of repentance for the forgiveness of sins. (Mark 1:4)

John was the one who would prepare the way for Jesus – he was preaching that the forgiveness of sins comes when we repent; turn around, change our thinking and look at God. He was pulling people in, towards Jesus:

And this was his message: "After me comes the one more powerful than I, the straps of whose sandals I am not worthy to stoop down and untie. I

baptise you with water, but he will baptise you with the Holy Spirit"
(Mark 1:7-8)

Surely, this should be the way that we walk on this earth, the way that we engage with other people: preaching the gospel, telling of God's love and bringing them into a relationship with Him, baptising them, all the while saying this: **this is who I am and this is what I am doing, but there is one that I represent, one who is in us and who goes before us, one who is the real deal**. We do things in the natural but, in His power, the Holy Spirit gets involved and things become much, much bigger than simply what we can do. Our role is to prepare the way for Jesus to come in and do His thing. Allow this to take the pressure off – your role is not to bring all of the people around you to Jesus, to transform them all into amazing people; but to prepare the way for God to come in and do his thing.

Awesome things begin to happen when we know who we really are. When we live out our identity as children of God, it brings glory to the God who created us. It means that we get to embark on this adventure of walking with God every day, allowing Him to work and seeing him do beautiful things through us.

Ready? Let's go!

CHAPTER ONE
I AM NOT…

When God made Adam and Eve, the first humans, we read in the Bible that He looked at all that He had made and He said: ***"it is good"***. God's creation was not just acceptable, not just a necessity, but good and perfect, because they were exactly as He had intended them to be. The Word said that we were made in His image - reflections of the God who created us, His character echoed in our character. Adam was put in a perfect garden that God had made, and it was good to be in; there were all kinds of trees that were pleasing to the eye and good for food. He had a responsibility in the garden, to work it and take care of it; God was entrusting man with His creation. That seems like a pretty sweet life to me, taking care of a garden that was perfect already, living in peace with the God who created me. There was freedom – freedom to enjoy any tree in the garden; and yet there was protection from the things that would cause harm:

The Lord God took the man and put him in the Garden of Eden to work it and take care of it. And the Lord God commanded the man, "You are free to eat from any tree in the garden, but you must not eat from the tree of the knowledge of good and evil, for when you eat from it you will certainly die." (Genesis 2:15-17)

But the enemy was sneaky, and knew how to tempt them: ***"You will not certainly die," the serpent said to the woman. "For God knows that when you eat of it your eyes will be opened, and you will be like God, knowing good and evil." (Genesis 3:4-5)*** The enemy was going against the things that God had said – "Are you sure? That's not true..." – but he was also trying to tempt them with something that they already were. He told them that if they ate from the tree they would become like God, but they already were like God: made in His image, and living with Him in the garden. "If you do this", he said, "you will be everything that you want to be – this will bring you closer to God, will make you a better person".

How often do we fall for this? How often do we waste our lives trying to live up to the expectations of others, or even living with a feeling of failure because we're not living up to the expectations that we think God has of us? You're not praying enough, you're not good enough, you mess up too often; and until you've prayed hard enough to earn His forgiveness, you're not good enough in His sight. This sounds right; we want to be right in God's eyes, and these are the things that we think we should be doing to be pleasing and acceptable to God. But the truth is, we already are good enough. We were created in His image; He looks at us and He calls us good, and because of Jesus, this is what He sees when He looks at us now. Because of Jesus, we ARE holy and blameless, we ARE children of God, we ARE forgiven for everything that we have ever done, and everything we will ever do - this was done on the cross, and there's nothing we can do to add to it.

There are no terms and conditions, no hidden extras, and no way that we can break the contract - He's already dealt with it all on the cross. He created you, and He is chasing after you. When we make this our starting point and live in this truth, it is His life and power that works through us, and we just get to be in awe at all He can do. Come as you are, and see God do great works in and through you, because you are His creation, whom He looks at and says *it is good*.

Insecurity and fear are killers of the joy that God has set inside us, and if we let them they have the power to knock us off our feet, and stop us realising the truth of who we are. But these are the words that God speaks over you: you are **good,** you are **holy and blameless,** you are **made in His image.** All too often our heads become foggy with other words that are thrown at us and the fears that creep in, but this is the truth: God loves you, because He loves you, because He loves you, because He created you and put you here, now. It was His choice. You are not a mistake, you are not forgotten, you are not alone. You are a child of the Most High God, who loves you, because you are you, and because you are His.

Words are one of the most powerful tools that we have at our disposal. They can be beautiful – they can twist and turn like a flowing water, bringing life to those that they pass – or they can bring death and destruction, knocking down those that stand in their way. They have such a powerful effect on our lives. Speaking to victims of abuse and slavery, I hear how the thing that has had the biggest lasting effect on their lives, more than the physical abuse, is the words – the verbal abuse, the way they were treated, the way they were made to feel about themselves. Words have the power make us feel worthless, and the intent behind the words that we use determines whether we bring light, or darkness, into situations. Verbal abuse stings because it cuts deep into our being; it pushes into our thought life and eventually changes the way that we speak about ourselves. Equally, words that are spoken over us with a positive intent have the power to inspire and encourage, and to change the way that we feel about ourselves from the inside out.

Typically we remember negative words that were spoken over us, and allow them to change the way we think about ourselves, much more than the positive words. It's in our wiring: the brain handles positive and negative information in different hemispheres. Negative emotions involve more thinking, and the information is processed more than positive ones; thus, we tend to ruminate more about unpleasant events – and use stronger words to describe them – than happy ones.

We tend to choose the words that we hear and allow to soak in to our being. Maybe at first, it's based on how we perceive ourselves, and then the words that we place on our lives become a lens – a filter that we use to see life and to hear the words of those around us. If you have an inherent belief that you are incompetent, you are going to be hyper-aware of what people might be thinking of you; you are going to assume that you are failing at the things that you are doing, and ultimately, you are not going to take the chances that you would take if you didn't have this belief. This filter can go unnoticed for most of our lives, or feel too big and too immovable to do anything about, but it has a massive impact on the way that we view the opportunities that come to us, and the way that we make decisions.

Often, the words that are put on our lives, either by ourselves or others, are based on our perceived performance; this invisible, unspoken standard that we are held to. In this pattern of needing to make the grade, do and say the right things, and not stick out, the words we put on our own identity come from whether we match up to these standards or not. This spirit of "not enough", if it is the core of how we perceive ourselves, has the power to limit us and keep us in bondage, holding us back from the fullness of all that God saw when He looked down at His creation and said "it is good".

Labels

In a world where God created all of us, uniquely and for a purpose, labels and stereotypes come in and limit our view of the world. Stereotypes are a fixed, generalised way of thinking about a group of people; teenagers, hipsters, old people, young people, students, big people, small people, chavs, townies, Muslims, Christians – these labels can all come with assumptions of what these people will be like, and we can generalise a huge group of people based on these assumptions. Stereotypes mean we ignore the differences between individual people; they make it easy for us to 'know' what someone is like, because they fit into a nice box. They affect the way that people see you, the way that people speak to you, and the way that we relate to each other. If labels are the filter through which others relate to you, the words that are thrown at you and the assumptions that are made about you can start to influence the way that you see yourself. If you're told you are something enough – over and over again – you start to **believe it**, and then you start to **accept it**, and then you start to **live like it**. Useless, useless, useless, useless, useless. Ugly, ugly, ugly, ugly, ugly. Unlovable, unlovable, unlovable, unlovable. Only good for one thing, only good for one thing, only good for one thing, only good for one thing, only good for one thing.

Stereotypes and labels have become a cultural norm. They are such a key part of the way that we relate to each other that we don't question them, we don't see a way of relating to each other differently; but one of the most dangerous things in our culture is simply doing things "the way we do things". Blindly doing things because they are "the way things are done" puts people in bondage; it oppresses the same people that have always been oppressed because nobody sees a different way of thinking about them. But you have the power to choose to be different; you can be the one who does not simply do things the way that they have always been done, who doesn't think about people and treat people in the same way as everyone else. Challenge things, think differently. Ask questions, ask why things happen, and decide whether you are going to go along with it, or not. As you go on this journey, breaking out of the boxes that you have been put in, dare yourself to look at others as human beings in the same way; not as the labels that the world has put on them, or the words that are spoken over them, or the things that you see when you first look at them: as the human being that they are.

There are some places in life where labels are helpful. I am a youth worker – that's my job title – so it's a helpful way to explain what I do to other people. *"What do you do, Heather?" "I'm a youth worker."* They have an idea of what a youth worker is in their head, and normally it's not too different from what I'm trying to explain, so it's a good way for me to communicate what my life looks like. Normally the conversation carries on and we expand on what this means – what does my working week look like? What kind of young people do I work with? What do I enjoy about my job? What do I find challenging? It very quickly goes deeper than the assumptions made around the label.

This label is great as a way of communicating what I do. It's great for me to keep what I'm doing in mind: my main priority today is to work with young people – it's in the title. But this label is not **who I am.** I am not a Youth Worker – I work as a youth worker. Finding my identity in being a youth worker could be absolutely fine, but what if suddenly I find that I don't have the opportunity to do youth work anymore, or I move on and try something new? Finding your identity in the things that you do only works as long as you are doing that thing – and puts you in danger of a serious identity crash when you're not doing it anymore. It's exactly the same, no matter what your job title is. If you are a painter, that's not **who you are,** it's what you do. If you're a teacher, it's not who you are; your identity is much bigger than teaching, and you teach.

It's so tempting for us to find our identity in what we do, because we spend so much of our life doing it; and usually, it's something that you're good at and you feel confident in. But what happens when you're suddenly not doing that thing anymore? Or you lose the ability to do it, or someone tells you that you're not very good at it? Then who are you? The answer is very simple, really, but can be hard to believe and take on for our own lives – **you are a child of God.** That's all He's asking for – before you do anything for Him, before you are anything for Him, you are His child and He is your Father. And to please our Father, there is no standard that we need to reach, there is no "enough" that we need to make sure that we are doing; we just need to fall into His arms, just as we are.

Rob

I've been working as a youth worker for a few years now, and one of the wonderful young people that I've had the honour to work with is a young lad called Rob*; a fourteen-year-old who lives in Cambridge, in one of the housing estates on the edge of the city. Cambridge is a very interesting city, with a real split between the wealth of the universities and the academic culture and the poverty of the housing estates and disadvantaged areas that surround it; these are areas that most people drive through every day, and yet they are a different world from the centre of Cambridge. This place has become a huge part of Rob's story. In reality, his prospects aren't looking great. He lives in a place where 27% of the children live below the poverty line – a huge increase on the rest of Cambridge – and 28% of homes in this area don't have anyone in employment.

Everything and everyone in Rob's world is telling him that he doesn't stand a chance; and this is the place that this fourteen-year-old kid is starting from. It is understandable why areas like this have such a huge crime rate – in March 2016, there were 110 reported crimes in that small area, and 40% of these were anti-social behaviour offences. A head-teacher in this area has said that unfortunately, most of his students will end up unemployed: that's just the way it is, he'll say. Talking to Rob, he feels like there's just no point: he isn't going to get anywhere, so why bother trying?

If you grow up with that voice telling you that you're probably going to end up unemployed, that you don't really stand a chance from the outset, then why would you bother? But that's not the truth. It's not the truth that the young people on that estate are unemployable - there are kids on that estate, Rob included, with hopes and dreams bigger than you can imagine, bigger than mine. They're not hopeless until somebody tells them that there's no hope. If they are allowed to, the stereotypes and labels that are put on Rob and his peers could keep them in a box, and completely limit their potential – but we all have a choice. I have the choice of whether I am going to talk to Rob in the same way as the rest of society has – as all the leaders in his life have – simply because that is the way that things are done; or whether I'm going to decide instead to encourage Rob and build him up, and tell him that there is a world that is bigger than the box that he has been put in.

Like each one of us, Rob has a history and a story. I love listening to him talk about the things that he has learnt as he has become the person that he is today. The area that he lives in and the people that are around him have had a huge influence on him: challenging him, helping him to grow, and being there for him. We can't write these things off, but our identity is not in where we are, who we are around or what has happened to us; our identity is found in being a child of God. Every one of us can live out of this identity, and we are all on a level playing field. Nothing that has come before affects our worth or value in this, but instead, we all start from the same place.

Chains

When circus elephants are young, they are contained to a certain area with a chain around their leg, which is then attached to a wooden peg in the ground. When they try to move, or break away, the chain cuts into their leg and hurts them, pulling them back to where they started. Eventually, they stop trying to move, because they know that any attempt won't work, and they will get hurt. If elephants are trained like this when they are young, and kept in captivity for their whole lives, as many circus elephants are, you can keep fully grown, mighty elephants still in the same way – tie a chain around their leg and attach it to a peg in the ground. The elephant has the strength and might to break free from their captivity, but they don't – why? Because they remember the times when they have tried to go and failed; they have been trained to think that they can't go anywhere. They remember the pain from the times they have tried before, and they do not move for fear of getting hurt again.

We all grow up looking up, thinking about what we want to do and where we want to go. But somewhere along the lines, the words that are spoken over us seem to put a chain around our leg and attach us to the ground where we are. We are trained on the "you can't do that"s, and the "you'll never be able to go there"s, and eventually we stop trying. Sometimes we try to do something, and we're knocked back by the people who tell us there's no point. Maybe we even fail because we don't have enough confidence in our own abilities, reinforcing the things that others say about us. But we have the might and power in us to break free from that chain around our leg. It won't be as painful as we think, but it's something new, something that we haven't done before. We can recognise what it is that is holding us back, recognise our own strength, and take the risk.

Sometimes, the beliefs that we have about ourselves are formed on the words that have been spoken over us, repeatedly, until they become a part of who we are. Useless, useless, useless, useless, useless, useless. Eventually you stop recognising the word for what it is – a lie – and you begin to accept it. Sometimes our beliefs about ourselves are formed on past experiences; most of our learning is based on bad experiences. We know that the stove is hot because we've been burnt, we know that falling hurts from the times that we've tried something and failed. Negative experiences reinforce what we can't do, and have the potential to sow fear in us, or dictate whether we will try something new. Even when our spirit leaps at the idea of something, our head quite often manages to shout it down and keep it from doing things for fear of failure. Negative experiences have the potential to become that chain around our leg, convincing us that we are stuck, despite our size or the might that we have.

So, let's break off some chains:

<ins>I Am Not a Failure</ins>

When something negative happens in our lives, when we mess up or try something that doesn't work, we are totally involved in it: our spirit, soul and body react and our brain kicks in and tells us not to do it again. These negative experiences reinforce what we can't do – when we weren't good enough, when we didn't match up – so then, the next time the opportunity comes up, our spirit might leap at the idea, but it can be easily talked down by our brain. The times that we fail can leave us feeling like a failure – and then, because we're a failure, we don't try again. When things are coming up that we could have a go at, our brain kicks in and tells us that we're a failure, and we don't attempt them for fear of things going wrong again. Maybe we've even been told that we're a failure – maybe this belief has been reinforced by the things that people have said about us. Maybe we've felt that we've had no option but to believe it was true, because there's been no-one telling us any different. But even if I'm the sole voice in your life telling you this right now, hear this: **you are not a failure**. Getting things wrong is an unavoidable part of life; but it is not how many times we fall that matters at all, as long as we get up one time more than we have fallen. Strength is found when we get back up, brush ourselves off, spend some time with our heavenly Dad, and give life another shot.

In the Bible, we read about a man called Abraham: he was a hero, and he's known now as the father of our faith. Throughout the Bible, we see God change the names of people who went through a radical transformation: he took 'Abram' and made him 'Abraham', a name to be proud of. The name Abram was no longer spoken over him, full of fear and insecurity and unbelief – instead, the name Abraham was one of faith.

The whole of Abraham's story is awesome, and we'll return to it later; but there's a point near the beginning of his story that radically changes the way that Abraham thinks about himself. Abram, as he was at this point, was having a bit of a moan at God. He was old, and he hadn't had any children, which was very important in that culture, and he had pretty much given up hope – he was moaning at God, and trying to find a solution himself. He said:

"Sovereign Lord, what can you give me since I remain childless?" "You have given me no children; so, a servant in my household will be my heir" (Genesis 15:2-3)

But God used that moment to give Abram a promise. He took him outside, and said, *"look up at the sky and count the stars – if indeed you can count them. So shall your offspring be."* Abram was moaning, he was trying to find his own solution, and he didn't think that God had come through for him – but this didn't affect the blessing that God gave him. He lived an awesome life. We read about Abraham all through the Bible – he was one of the key players – and it says that he *"believed God, and it was credited to him as righteousness." (Romans 4:3)* Abraham is remembered as one of the heroes of the faith, just because he believed that what God said about him was true.

Abraham and his wife were both old, and they had failed to achieve something that was hugely important to them. They couldn't see a way out of their situation in the moment, and they were desperately searching for ways to make it happen – *maybe one of my servants can be my heir*. But in that moment, God intervened, and gave Abram a promise of all that He was capable of doing: and all that Abram needed to do was believe that what God said was true.

We catch up with Abraham later on in the Bible, when Paul is remembering him as one of the heroes of our faith. This is what Paul says about Abraham:

Against all hope, Abraham in hope believed and so became the father of many nations, just as it had been said to him, "So shall your offspring be." Without weakening in his faith, he faced the fact that his body was as good as dead—since he was about a hundred years old—and that Sarah's womb was also dead. Yet he did not waver through unbelief regarding the promise of God, but was strengthened in his faith and gave glory to God, being fully persuaded that God had power to do what he had promised." (Romans 4:18-21)

Abraham felt and acknowledged what was going on around him – he and his wife were old, and biology said that they would not be able to have children! He acknowledged this without weakening his faith in the God who works miracles, and **against all hope, he in hope believed.** When his circumstances told him that there was no hope, he held on to hope in God, and fully believed that God had the power to do what He had promised. He had a promise from God, and that is what he hung his faith on.

Moments of failure seem like the biggest deal when we are in the moment. But Failure is not your name, and it is not what you need to live under, because you are a child of God. You have the most incredible future ahead of you. You are a child of God, and your Dad is the coolest Dad of all Dads – He's got your name written on His hand. You are going to live a great life, full of amazing moments that you can't even imagine yet. Your job is not to be the most amazing, incredible, talented, sparkly person and get everything right all the time. We can't get everything right all the time – but we're not supposed to. We're supposed to believe that the things that God says about us are true, and *that* is what makes us amazing and sparkly in His eyes.

When a child is learning to ride a bike, they don't have to worry about falling or failing; their Dad is alongside them with his arms outstretched, and if they do fall, he'll catch them. Eventually, the Dads must step back and watch while the child has a go on their own – but even if they fall, their Dad is ready to come along and pick them up.

I lift my eyes to the mountains – where does my help come from? My help comes from the Lord, the maker of heaven and earth. He will not let your foot slip – he who watches over you will not slumber. (Psalm 121:1-3)

You are not a failure – you are a child of God.

<u>I Am Not Unlovable.</u>

Life can throw some serious stuff at us sometimes, and relationships are one of the areas that have the potential to make you feel absolutely rubbish about yourself. Essentially, when we're rejected in this area, it feels like someone is saying "you're just not good enough. I'd rather spend my life, or my time, or my affection, with someone else". Suddenly, we question everything about ourselves – what is it about me? What's wrong with me? Why aren't I good enough? Eventually, we can start to live in that place – there's something wrong with me, I'm not good enough, I'm ugly, I'm too clingy. I'm pretty much unlovable. Or maybe the issue goes way deeper than that, and we've grown up with this deep-seeded belief that we're completely unlovable. Just as when you're told something over and over again you start to believe it, if you're never told something – if there's a complete absence of something – it's very hard to believe it. If you go through life never being told that you're loved, that you're worthy of being loved, then the concept will be completely foreign to you and it will actually be easier to believe the opposite. The first hurdle to believing that we are loved by God can be believing that we are worthy of love in the first place.

You are worthy of love, and you are deeply loved, whether you are in a relationship or not. This is what God says about you:

"On the day when I act," says the Lord Almighty, "they will be my treasured possession. I will spare them, just as a father has compassion and spares his son who serves him" (Malachi 3:17)

There's something important about the word 'spare' here: a meaning much deeper than the one which may originally come to mind. The word used in the language that this passage was originally written in was ***chamal***, which, at its root, actually means to have concern for, to desire, to have compassion for and to become responsible for. This is the promise that God is making for His people: **I will desire them, just as in compassion a man desires his son.**

You are His treasured possession, and it is you that He is seeking after. Let this be a reminder to you: God is on your case. He's chasing after you. He wants a relationship with you – He's calling you His treasured possession, He has compassion for you and He desires you in the same way that a father desires his son.

This desire that God has for you has nothing to do with who you are, how "good" you are perceived to be, or the things that you do. We can see the love that God has for His people all through the Bible, but one of my favourites was a woman called Rahab. She was one of the key players: she saved the lives of two people that God had sent into her land by hiding them in her house, and then telling them which way to run. She made it into the family tree of Jesus; she was the mother of a man called Boaz, who was the father of a man called Obez… and somewhere down that line was J.C. She risked her life to save the lives of the two men.

Here's the start of Rahab's story, when we meet her:

> *Joshua son of Nun secretly sent out from Shittim two men as spies: "Go. Look over the land. Check out Jericho." They left and arrived at the house of a harlot named Rahab and stayed there. The king of Jericho was told, "We've just learned that men arrived tonight to spy out the land. They're from the People of Israel." The king of Jericho sent word to Rahab: "Bring out the men who came to you to stay the night in your house. They're spies; they've come to spy out the whole country." The woman had taken the two men and hidden them. She said, "Yes, two men did come to me, but I didn't know where they'd come from. At dark, when the gate was about to be shut, the men left. But I have no idea where they went. Hurry up! Chase them—you can still catch them!" (She had actually taken them up on the roof and hidden them under the stalks of flax that were spread out for her on the roof.) So the men set chase down the Jordan road toward the fords. As soon as they were gone, the gate was shut."*
>
> *(Joshua 2:1-7, MSG[1])*

These men had come into Jordan to take over the land and use it as God had told them to – but they were being hunted down by the king, and their lives were in danger. Rahab took them into her home and gave them a place to stay, and then protected them when the king's men came knocking on the door, before sending them safely on their way. She was a important player in this story.

But there was something that you wouldn't expect. **Rahab was a prostitute**. God used a prostitute. He could have protected His men in any number of other ways, but He chose to send them to a brothel to find safe-

---

[1] The Message Bible

ty. I sometimes wonder what reaction Rahab would get if she walked into a church in Britain today; would she be warmly accepted, or would she get weary looks and be treated differently? Rahab was the last person that you would expect to be in the Bible, especially in Jesus' family tree – why didn't God use someone else?

Here's why: **Rahab had a good heart.** This is what God saw; not that she was a prostitute, but that she had a heart for God and His people. This is what mattered in the end; it was because of her heart that she saved the two men from being killed. Because of what she did, Rahab's story became a part of God's story. She wasn't a priest, or a religious leader – she was pretty much the opposite. But she's the one in the family tree of Jesus. God used the last person that you would expect. I'm so thankful for this – I'm thankful that God doesn't just use the priests and the religious leaders and the people who get it "right". The world would have told Rahab that she was totally unlovable; that she was just too messy, that she had screwed up too many times and that she wasn't worthy of love. But she had a good heart, she acted with the best intentions, and she had God's **favour.**

Just like Rahab, God does not love you because you are a good person and you do all the right things; and, equally, He doesn't not love you when you mess up. God sees your heart, and He loves your heart; your heart that is flawless, holy, blameless – because of what Jesus has done. There were three things about Rahab that made her a force to be reckoned with, which can be just as true for you and me. Firstly, Rahab had **faith** – she said to the men, *"I know that the Lord has given you this land." (Joshua 2:8)* We do not have to live up to any standards, or save ourselves by what we do; we just need to know that there is a God who saves us. That's all salvation is – recognising the things that God has done for us through Jesus. Secondly, Rahab **spoke** of how good God is – she said He is *"God in heaven above and on the earth below." (Joshua 2:11)* She knew who she was talking about! And thirdly, Rahab **loved** the people around her: when the two men promised that they would protect her for what she had done for them, she said, *"swear to me that you will also show kindness to my family." (Joshua 2:12)* She didn't just want that promise for herself, but wanted to make sure that her family were protected too.

As a response to who God is, and the love that He has for us, we all have the capacity for these three things; to have faith, to speak of how good God is, and to love the people around us – and these things come from our heart. Everything that we do, and everything that we say, comes from our heart: the Bible calls it the "spring of life". So if we have a good heart, the things that we do and the way we speak are going to be good. If you know God, you have the Holy Spirit inside you. And that means that your heart is

covered by God's heart; you have the love of God inside of
you. **Awesome**, right? The grace of God means that my heart is covered by what Jesus did on the cross – God sees me as clean and pure. You are lovable, and you are so loved by God; not because you are good enough, or because of the way you look, or the things that you can do, but because He has given you a good heart.

> ***And by that will, we have been made holy, through the sacrifice of the body of Jesus Christ once for all. (Hebrews 10:10)***

So, because God's grace and Christ's sacrifice covers you, and He sees you as pure, God is dealing with your **heart** – not your actions! He doesn't even keep a record of the things that you have done, and He covers everything that you will ever do; God sees your heart and He loves it.

You are not unlovable – you are clean and pure, and God loves you not because of your actions, but because He created you.

I Am Not Alone

Story time: It's 10:09 am on a Friday morning, and we're stuck in traffic. The meeting that we're supposed to be at started nine minutes ago, and yet we're still crawling over the busiest road in Cambridge, in bumper to bumper traffic. Now – I'm not a "morning person" at the best of times, and as I haven't had my two coffees yet, I'm a little bit grumpy.

I turn the radio up a little bit, and rest my head on my window as we come to another stop at the traffic lights.

"If we could just hit *every* set of traffic lights, that would be fantastic" I mutter, sarcastically.

We eventually move past the lights, shuffle over a roundabout, and just as the traffic begins to clear… we hit a red light. Sure enough, we see every single set of lights turn red down that half-mile stretch of road – just in time for us to have to come to a stop.

"I think He heard you," chips in my super-helpful friend, sat in my passenger seat.

There are times in my life when it's super-obvious that God is walking along next to me – I can chat away in His ear, and I know that I don't need to explain to Him what's going on with me, because He already knows – He walked it with me. Times when my life echoes the walk of the man in the *Footprints in the Sand* poem – He's walking next to me, and when those footprints disappear, it's because He's carrying me.

This is who God really is. He's watching me; laughing with me when I say something silly, jumping up and down in joy when I look to Him, holding His hand out for me to grab. He's dancing with me when I'm spinning round with joy, jumping round my kitchen to cheesy 90's pop music. And when I royally mess up, He's crouched down next to me, picking up the pieces and keeping me company on the floor. My God sees my heart, the things that nobody else gets to see.

Those times are great – skipping through a field of daisies with Him, the sun shining, no storms in sight. But life isn't always like that. There are times when the winds come and it feels like my hand is torn away from His, and instead of a field of daisies, I'm sat in a desert.

Here's what God does when His children are in the desert:

He found him out in the wilderness, in an empty, windswept wasteland. He threw his arms around him, lavished attention on him, guarding him as the apple of his eye. He was like an eagle hovering over its nest, overshadowing its young. Then spreading its wings, lifting them into the air, teaching them to fly. (Deuteronomy 32:10-12, MSG)

Because here's the thing: **in the moments when it doesn't feel like He's right there next to you, He's the eagle swooping overhead, guarding you.** You don't mess with an eagle when it's protecting its young – no-one's getting near that nest. Then when the danger's gone, He swoops down, lifts you up into the air and teaches you to fly again. **Sometimes we need moments of resting in His protection, so we can have the power to fly again.**

Also, this has nothing to do with where we're at or what we're doing. Even when I royally mess up, or feel like I'm not doing the right thing, He's still going to sweep me up and help me to fly again.

Whoever dwells in the shadow of the Most High will rest in the shadow of the Almighty. (Psalm 91:1)

The word "dwells" literally means to sit – sit in God's shadow, and He'll protect you. And the amazing thing is that this doesn't need any work from me at all – sitting is the easiest thing to do.

When we're in that desert place sometimes it feels like we need to dig ourselves out: this is **my** mess, I'm the one that got myself here – if only I could sort myself out. But all God asks to do is sit in His presence and He'll sweep us up on His wings. It's that easy! We're the apple of His eye – we're His favourite – and there's nothing that we can do to mess that up.

God is not ignoring you. When I made a sarcastic comment and suddenly every light turned red, I had a bit of a strop with God. "So, you heard *that*? Every light is turning red right now, and yet *this* situation is still going on for me? *Seriously?*"

But there's nothing more watchful than an eagle over their young – while He's swooping overhead, nothing can get close. I'll probably never know the things that God was protecting me from while He was up there – and all I need to do is let Him sweep me up and teach me to fly. The Bible says that *"those who hope in the Lord will renew their strength. They will soar on wings like eagles; they will run and not grow weary." (Isaiah 40:31)* When you're soaring, the burdens are gone – when you're running, there's nothing on you to hold you back.

And I also know that God's got a sense of humour; He's laughing with me. By the time we reached the car park, I had breathed out, sung along with the radio for a while, and come to terms with the fact that the world isn't against me. I didn't need saving – I needed my Dad to remind me that He hears me and that He's with me.

To be able to soar, all you have to do is sit. I want to be a part of what He's doing, but **grace** means that everything that I'm trying to do has already been done – God dealt with it all on the cross. When I stress, when I strive and try to battle on my own, I'm trying to take that away from Him. We can hold on to His promises.

"The Lord will fight for you; you need only to be still." (Exodus 14:14)

You are not alone – God is with you, and He's protecting you.

Moving On

The first step is to recognise which of the beliefs we have about ourselves have come from either *words* spoken over us, or from our *past experiences*; we can break these things off and decide to believe the truth of what God says about us. I'd encourage you to take some time to think about what these things are for you. What are the words that have been spoken over you; what boxes have you been put in? Quiet. Boring. Chav. Posh. Fat. Anorexic. Weird. Outsider. Not good enough. Write them down, put them out there; they're not the truth, so there's nothing to fear in speaking them out. Think about the words that you've chosen; imagine if this was spoken over you every day - imagine if it was all that you told yourself. Not good enough. Not good enough. Not good enough. Not good enough. Over time, our head shouts over our heart so much that we begin to believe that it is true. You are so much more than what the world says you are. The rest of this book is going to begin to explore everything that we **are** when we find our identity in truth - it's a message that is so different from everything that the world tells us, and it will bring you more freedom than you can imagine.

When I've spoken about this with young people around the country, we've had a fun, crazy minute that we've found helpful in deciding to move on from believing these lies about ourselves: I'd encourage you to give it a go. Find the words that you wrote down, or write down the things that you want to get rid of, then pick the loudest, craziest rock song you can find, blast it for thirty seconds and destroy that piece of paper. Rip it up, stamp on it, throw it, whatever it takes. Make this your decision that you are not going to let these things define you anymore, and let's start the rest of this crazy journey.

A self-help book would tell you that we're a product of all the people that we have hung out with, all of the decisions we have made; all the adventures we have had and everything that we learnt through them. It would tell you that on our skin we wear every word that has been spoken over us; everything we've ever been told is true about ourselves. We're all of the friends that have encouraged us, and everyone that has tried to beat us down.

But I'm not sure that that's entirely true. Yes, those things can influence us, can mold us into the person that we become – if we give them the power. But when we know Jesus, it's not about how long the chain is that is holding us back; no matter many words have been spoken over us to encourage or discourage us – we are the circus elephant with the power inside us to break free from the chain. If the truth of who we are is in us, the words that are spoken over us – good or bad – have no power at all.

As we walk through life, so much of what we do comes from trying to live up to the person that we want the world to see us as. It's easy to create this person, this character, and often the way that we speak and act comes from that person, rather than who we really are. Maybe they're slightly cooler than we think we are, slightly more intelligent, more funny; maybe, they're slightly closer to God than we think we are.

Through a lot of stupid decisions and lessons learned, I've realised that me being King of my own life does not work. When I try to do this, there are decisions that I can't be trusted to make: I do things to try and live up to this person that I've created, and ultimately it fails because that's not who I really am. In that there's this fear; this fear that one day people are going to realise I'm a fake, a fraud. That fear leads me into the decisions that I make and dictates the way that I live.

Right at the start of Jesus' ministry, before He did anything that we read about in the Bible, Jesus was baptised. And when He was baptised, it says that God looked down on Him and said *"this is my son, whom I love, and with him I am well pleased"*. Before He did anything, before He could have earned God's love, His Father looked down on Him, loved Him and was pleased with Him. It's the same for you and me – God looks down on us and says *"this is my son, this is my daughter, whom I love. And with them I am well pleased"*.

This is the truth; that you are God's child, whom He loves, and with whom He is well pleased. But often our lives are formed around deep-seated lies, based on these things that we have believed. They're formed around the things that have hurt us, the times that we've failed, the things that people have spoken over us that have kept us in captivity. But here's what God says: you are His child, whom He loves, and with whom He is well pleased – not based on what you can do or how good you are, but just who you are. When we live in this place of being enough just because of who we are, we have the power to break free from the chains that hold us. From that point, Jesus went out and spent his life healing the sick, preaching the gospel, doing amazing things. His starting point was in His identity – *"this is my son, whom I love, and with whom I am well pleased."*

Let's Start the Journey

We're about to go on an awesome journey together, of working out who we are in God and letting that leak out into the way that we live and love others. But to start with, we need to leave this stuff behind – we need to make a conscious decision that we're going to leave everything that the world has told us to believe about ourselves here, and we're going to be open to hearing what God says about us.

Write it down, get it out, leave it here. Write down the words, and things that have been spoken over you on scraps of paper or card. Destroy those pieces of paper. Rip it up, stamp on it, screw it up, throw it away – and use this as an opportunity to make a decision that those words do not define you anymore.

Questions for Reflection

1. *What is your "I Am Not…"?*

2. *Where has this lie been a chain or blockage in your life?*

3. *How does it feel, or how would it feel, to tear up that label and leave it here?*

CHAPTER TWO
I AM GOOD

We all have a story. It may not begin with Once Upon a Time, and end with Happy Ever After right now; but we all have a story to share, a journey that we went on to get to the person that we are today. We all continue this growth and transformation for the rest of our lives, so the story is very much not over yet; but in the natural, the person that we are standing as, right here in this moment, is a product of everything that has come before. We tell our stories to try and explain the person that we are to the world. When we know Jesus, we call this a testimony – a story of the things that God has done in us to get us to the point where we now stand. Our stories are powerful – they have the power to influence and inspire, to encourage others that their story is not over yet. Hearing the stories of other people tells us that **it is not over yet**. If they got through the things that they were going through, then so can we. The place that we are in now is not the end of the story. We're not stuck in this place for the rest of our life; as people, we are constantly changing and transforming, learning about the world and our place in it. Life is constantly getting bigger, and hearing the stories of others tells us that it does not stop here.

Pete's Story

My friend Pete is the most incredible example of a man of God, living out his identity as a child of God. His story is not an easy one, but his decision to follow God drastically changed the path that his life was going on, and he tells his story in order that it will give others hope in their situations, as he found hope in his.

As I write this, he's sat across the table from me, finishing off the revision for the last exams of his degree, and chatting to me all about his heart for going after the exciting plans that God has for him. If I was to describe him in one word, it would be faithful; he's faithful in serving, a loyal friend, and generally just a top guy. In my life, he's been a consistent presence of love and support, and he's constantly pointing me to God – but, as he describes, he's been on a journey to get to the dreams that God has put on his heart.

"I grew up in a Christian family" he says to me, sipping his fancy coffee from his fancy coffee cup. *"I went to church every Sunday, and I think I always believed in God. Everything that I learnt as a kid has been a strong foundation that has stayed with me. I became a Christian when I was seven, in kids work at church. I didn't see much of a difference between church and school – they were both places where I just learnt things that I knew were true.*

When I was ten my parents started chatting to me about baptism – and I began to ask God to fill me with the Holy Spirit. God gave me a Bible verse, and from there I started to learn how to hear from God. I got baptised later that year, and loved church.

When I was about twelve, my parents stopped going to that church, and at this point I was only going about once a month. I began to realise that my faith is my responsibility: if I want to worship, I need to make space for it – I didn't want to be spoon-fed. From this point, I've let the Spirit lead me.

When I was about sixteen, I found that I didn't really have any community. I felt God tell me to go to a particular church in Cambridge, so I went and joined the youth group. Around this time, I started sixth form, and struggled with comparing myself to other people. I was always the quiet kid, and struggled with self-confidence, and that led me to looking to all the wrong places to sort that out.

I had bad relationships, got involved with drinking with friends, and started to find that church people can let you down. I saw that people in the church put on a face to make them look better than everyone else – but people in the world loved me more. I found more acceptance with my friends from college, who didn't judge me for the things I was doing, and they didn't pretend to be any better.

This is what I took with me when I went to uni. I'd spend most days getting drunk, and even high with my friends – because I knew that it would make me a part of things. It worked – I had a lot of friends as a result. But all the while, I knew that whatever I thought of Christians, God was still good, and I knew that there were some Christians that did get it right.

I never lost my faith. Every night I'd come in drunk, go to my room and pray it would never happen again – but I couldn't resist the peer pressure. I knew that the way I was living wasn't the way that God was wanting me to – it wasn't what I was supposed to be doing.

I never gave up on church. I'd go out on a Saturday night, get back at

5am, get up at 8am and go to church – I didn't want to let that part of my life go. Eventually I made the decision to drop out – I didn't want to do the course any more, and I couldn't carry on with the way I was living. The two things that really meant something to me were God and music – and that's what I wanted to do."

I didn't know Pete when he was at university, but as he described his story to me, I tried to picture what he would have been like as a friend. I get the privilege of knowing the awesome guy that sits in front of me: he's finishing his degree in music production; I met him at church, where he's fully plugged in, leading worship, heading up the P.A team and helping out with the youth work. He's looking at plans for his future – thinking about how he's going to carry on pursuing the path of God and music.

This is not a lecture advising you not to go near drugs and alcohol, and to behave a certain way; that is not the point here, and our relationship with God is about so much more than the way we behave. Instead, Pete struggled because of where he was looking to find his value: he felt valued because of the things that he did, rather than who he was. But when God looked at Pete, He wasn't scolding him for the things that he was doing; God looks at Pete and sees His Son, whom He loves, and with whom He is well pleased.

Pete decided that what God said about him was more important that what the world said about him. At university, he says, he believed that he was valuable: he had a lot of friends, he went out a lot, he was a fun person to be around. He was a part of something bigger than himself – something that we all crave – because he behaved in a way that helped him to fit in with everyone else; he got drunk and high, he got into relationships, he went out. And, over time, he found his identity in these things: he was Pete, the fun guy to go out with; why would he act any differently? The decision to drop out of university was brave, and potentially changed the trajectory of his entire life: rather than carrying on living in a way that gained affirmation and acceptance from everyone around him, he took a step out and thought about who he really wanted to be.

When we hear stories like Pete's, we realise that we have the power to break free from things in the same way as he did. Pete, although being incredibly talented, inspiring and kind, is just a normal person; he hasn't got any extra holiness or super-ability to do things better than us. His power was in the way that he made the small decisions, which influenced the bigger picture.

You have the power to break free from having to be the person that the world tells you that you should be. You have the power, like Pete, to not change your behaviour to fit the expectation that is put on you, to not base your identity on what people think of you, but to look to God for your identity. This power is not found in our own strength, but in believing the truth that God created you, that He redeemed you, that He loves you and that He's so pleased with you; and this power makes the biggest difference to the way that we see ourselves, and the way that we walk out our lives.

Writing a New Story

Stories tell of everything that has come before, and go some way towards helping us understand the person that sits in front of us. But this is not the end of the story. While we might feel like we are a product of everything that has happened to us and all the words spoken over us, this is not the truth: the Word says that when we believe Jesus, we become new creations. We have the opportunity to say "goodbye" to the person that we were, to everything that has come before, and to write a new story in our identity in Christ. This is what the Bible says about us:

So from now on we regard no one from a worldly point of view. Though we once regarded Christ in this way, we do so no longer. Therefore, if anyone is in Christ, the new creation has come: The old has gone, the new is here! (2 Corinthians 5:16-17)

When we say "yes" to Jesus, when we accept the salvation that He gives us, we become included in Him. We're covered by Him: all of our sin, and shame, and baggage is gone, replaced by Jesus and His goodness. In that moment of accepting forgiveness and knowing that Christ died for you, your old self died, and Jesus came to live in you. The truth of this brings us freedom: God has made us holy and blameless, and free from accusation. We are marked in Him with a seal, and who we are is covered by who He is. This is all that salvation is – it's saying: "yes please!" and acknowledging that Christ died for you.

Everything that we have ever done, and everything that we will ever do, is forgiven, because of God's grace:

In him we have redemption through his blood, the forgiveness of sins, in accordance with the riches of God's grace. (Ephesians 1:7)

We're forgiven, and we're not under guilt or shame, but under the *riches of God's grace* – He has forgiven us because we are His, and He loves us. He wants to know people, He wants to save people into a relationship with Him. All it takes is a decision to say yes; and when we do, this grace brings us life, and joy, and peace overflowing. When we say yes, our identity is not found in the things that we have done, or our failings, or the things that we have earned in our own effort, but it is found in the riches of His love, which give us everything that we need. That's all you need to do: get your eyes off yourself – your old self – and look at Jesus and all that He is, because that is what you're hidden in. All that He has, we have; all that He does, so do we.

We are therefore Christ's ambassadors, as though God were making his appeal through us. We implore you on Christ's behalf: Be reconciled to God. God made him who had no sin to be sin for us, so that in him we might become the righteousness of God. (2 Corinthians 5:20-21)

To be made righteous literally means to be made what you ought to be. That's what happened when Jesus died on the cross – He took all your sin, all of your **old creation**, onto Himself, so that we might be hidden in Him, and be everything that we were created to be. If you are in Christ, there's nothing between you and God; you and God walk together. This is all that salvation is: as the Church, we've added things that we must do to be saved, words that we must say, moments where we must put our hand up in the right church service at the right time, but here's the truth:

And you also were included in Christ when you heard the message of truth, the gospel of your salvation. When you believed, you were marked in him with a seal, the promised Holy Spirit, who is a deposit guaranteeing our inheritance until the redemption of those who are God's possession – to the praise of his glory. (Ephesians 1:13-14)

There's nothing here about putting your hand up at the right moment, saying the right words, having to confess every sin, even having to be sorry – there is no condemnation in Christ Jesus, and guilt and shame is not from Him. Instead, salvation is about accepting the things that Christ has already done for you: we hear the word of truth, and we believe – and then we're marked in Him with a seal. That's all it takes!

We get to be Christ's ambassadors – this is life with Jesus, getting to walk with Him every day of our lives, so that others might see the truth of who He is. This isn't religion, it isn't duty: it's a relationship with the one who saves us, and walks every step with us, bringing us peace and joy beyond measure. This is the promise that God gives us:

You will keep in perfect peace those whose minds are steadfast, because they trust in you. Trust in the Lord forever, for the Lord, the Lord himself, is the rock eternal" (Isaiah 26:3-4)

When we look around us, our circumstances can wobble; but He, as the rock, will keep our mind steadfast. And this is a promise: He **will** keep us in perfect peace if we choose to take our mind off our own circumstances, and look at Him.

Breaking Free

I went for a walk with God at one point last year. I have the privilege of living in Cambridge, which is full of beautiful rivers and hills and narrow streets to wander down with a coffee. I was walking down the river, looking up at the tall colleges lit up in the darkness – and to be honest, in my head, I was yelling at God a little bit. That day had been stressful, and confusing, and I felt that I was totally within my rights to have a bit of a strop at Him. I was just getting to the end of my third excellent point about why that day had been so awful, when I heard that little voice, almost audible, but as if it was whispering straight into my ear: *"Why are you yelling? I'm right here."*

That voice stopped me in my tracks a little bit. I'd been yelling at God, because He's big and strong, and can see everything, and frankly He can handle it. But suddenly I was taken back to the moment when I realised that God isn't just some Morgan Freeman type character, sitting on a cloud and looking down at me, but He's a person, who's walking alongside me. I suddenly realised that I didn't need to explain what had happened to Him – He was there.

I don't have time for this idea of God that religion requires me to keep in line with. I don't have time for following rules and doing the right thing, just in case the big guy in the sky might get me. My God is a person, He's with me. He feels the pain that I feel, He laughs with me when I laugh. And I think, a lot of the time, he's chuckling at the silly things that I do, head in His hand.

But actually, my experience of life with God has been much more like a dance. When I was younger (cough… and now), I loved films like the Princess Diaries, or A Cinderella Story: classics – the girl gets to wear a pretty dress, and at the end she gets to dance with Prince Charming. Surrounded by stars. With confetti falling on them. That's what life with God is like; except He's a much better dancer than Prince Charming. Life with Him is about intimacy, spinning round, closeness with the One who made me. There are dips, twists and turns in the dance – moments where we might have to change direction; but that's not an issue, it's just part of the dance. If I start to fall, He just swoops me back up in His arms, and we carry on with the dance. And I don't even need to worry about where we're going; in a dance, you just feel the tiny motions to know where He wants you to go, and it's easy to follow them. An intimate relationship with our Father is the starting point of knowing our identity and living out with it. Faith that is based on religion will join in with the world's voices, telling you you're not good enough; telling you that God's love for you is based on what you do and that the things that you are doing are making God love you less. But we can have faith that's based on a relationship with our Father who loves us so much and wants a relationship; instead of being stern and cross with us, He treats us with loving kindness. All though history, God has had so much tender love for the people that He created. To the Israelites, He said:

It was I who taught Ephraim to walk, taking them by the arms; but they did not realise it was I who healed them. I led them with cords of human kindness, with ties of love. To them I was like one who lifts a little child to the cheek, and I bent down to feed them. (Hosea 11:3-4)

The God that said this looks, to me, like a father, bending down to show kindness and love to his children; so different to the image of that old man sat on the cloud. It speaks of a God teaching His children to walk, filled with tenderness and grace – not tutting at them when they get it wrong. He humbled Himself to bend down and feed the people; even people that had become arrogant and turned away from Him. His children were hurt and He responded as any father would – by bending down and comforting them. We're going to go on to look more at the story of the Israelites later in this book; it's a beautiful love story of God and His people.

When God calls His people, it is with kindness and love. This picture of a parent teaching a child to walk is filled with so much tenderness and grace, bending down to feed them, leading them so gently. You can't teach a child to walk without getting down on their level, without talking to them gently, without giving them help and guidance.

Children of God; Inherently Good

We are descendants of the people of Israel – the people that we read about in the Old Testament, who began a love story with the Father that has continued, and that we are still a part of now. We are a part of this same story – like the people of Israel, we are God's people, and He loves us with this same tenderness. The Bible says that when we know Christ, we become children of God:

Now if we are children, then we are heirs – heirs of God and co-heirs with Christ. (Romans 8:17)

God is not this far-away man, sat on a cloud. God is my Father – He bends down to me, He picks me up when I fall. And what's more; this isn't a chore to God – He gets *joy* from loving me!

Think about the difference in the relationship between a slave and a master, and a father and son. Slaves don't know their master's business, they're not a part of the family, they do the work simply out of duty. But sons have a relationship with the father, and they have a share in their father's inheritance. We are not slaves who do not know our Master, we are children who can have an intimate and personal relationship with our Father. This is where our identity is: before being a friend, a daughter, a student, a youth worker, a brother or a sister – we are a child of the God who created us. We're not just God's servants, and the good news is that we don't have to do anything to earn God's love. He created you, and He loves the person that He created.

So, a key part in beginning this journey to knowing our identity in Christ and letting it leak out into our whole lives is a realisation that because of our identity as a child of God, we are, **inherently, a good person**. The things that we looked at in the last chapter – the words that have been spoken over us, the things that we have done and the guilt and the shame that we might feel because of our past – have no power over us as a new creation: the old has gone, and the new is here!

Take a moment to thank God for making you new, for the new birth that you have because of what Jesus did on the cross – and then make the choice that you are no longer going to live as the old person, but that you're going to step into the new creation that God has made you.

This is not a one-off choice that you never need to think about again; it's an ongoing decision that we're not going to look at our circumstances, or what we feel like, or what the world is telling us about ourselves, but that we're going to look to God and the truth of what He says about us.

The Faith Gap

When we're living in Christ, nothing is on us: we don't have any needs, because God is our provider, and has given us everything that we need. We don't have any sickness, because God is our healer, and by His wounds we **are** healed – present tense (Isaiah 53:5)! As He is, so are you – everything that Jesus has, so do we. Get your eyes off of you, and your circumstances, and look at Him and the truth of what He has done for you.

Although this shouldn't be difficult, it is, somehow. We live in this tension of a gap between what we read in the Bible, what we know to be true, what God says about us; and what our lives physically look like day-to-day. God has healed all of our sickness and iniquities, and yet someone has terminal cancer. God is our provider and has given us everything that we need, and yet someone's in debt and can't afford to eat.

We plug this gap with **faith.** The decision to speak one over the other, and to believe that what the Word says is absolute truth. It's that easy – at some point, we must make the decision that what the Bible says is true, no matter what our circumstances look like. This isn't about feeling – our feelings lie to us. It's about knowing that His word is true.

The Word says that without faith it is impossible to please God (Hebrews 11:16) – therefore, we should always be looking for opportunities to practice our faith. And here's the thing about faith: **faith only stands from the moment we pray until the moment we see something happen.** Faith stands from the moment we lay our hands on the sick man and pray healing over him until the moment we see the healing come to pass. It stands from the moment you lift a request to God, and believe in faith that something will happen, until you see that thing happen. If you pray and see something happen straight away, very little faith is required – it was only required for the time of waiting between praying and seeing the thing happen. If we ask God for something that we already have the money in the bank for, with a little bit of shuffling, very little faith is required. It's not possible for something to be both a present reality, and a promise – if we have it already then we don't need to have faith for it.

Our issue comes when we don't see the present reality worked out in our lives. We know that God is our healer and that every sickness was defeated when Jesus died on the cross, and yet we have this ongoing sickness in our lives. Maybe sometimes, we are afraid to ask God for something because we think that if it doesn't happen, it will damage our faith in some way. Afraid to ask God to heal you, just in case He doesn't do it.

Our brain is programmed on our past experiences. When a child touches a hot stove and burns themselves, their brain will tell them not to do it again, because it hurt them. Most of our learning is based on negative experiences, which generally have more of a long-term effect than the positive experiences: when we're stung, when we get hurt, we learn not to try that thing again. Negative experiences reinforce what we can't do.

So when something comes up that requires us to exercise faith, although our spirit might be leaping, it can be talked down by our own head. We look at what we see around us, and the truth of what Jesus has done for us doesn't seem to fit.

But truth is truth is truth, and truth stands on its own. Our experience of reality is based on our perception. Our experience of reality can change depending on how wobbly our perception is, but truth never changes; that's what makes it truth. The truths that Jesus taught still stand, but the "realities" that we experience in the world, or even what the Church teaches, can change.

Faith stands from the moment we pray until we see something happen. So believing the things that Jesus has already done for us on the cross doesn't take a lot of faith; it's already been done. Instead, it's a matter of choosing to believe that it is true. We need to learn to trust the truth so much that our perception submits to it; then we won't be disorientated, we won't wobble. And when that feeling of disorientation comes over us, we need to be able to say, "I know what this feels like, I know what my reality is saying right now, but **this** is the truth".

The other point at which we need to use faith, more than simply believing that what God says about us is true, is in taking action; stepping into the things that God has asked us to do, and believing in the promises that God has made. Asking God for things when we already have enough money in the bank for does not require us to exercise a lot of faith; but asking God for something extraordinary takes faith.

This is where we face opposition: people around us telling us that it can't be done, telling us to be realistic, that we're going too far. But this is it – if you can't see it, it requires walking by faith. Make a decision that the things that people say will not wear you down; the more that people around you say that it can't be done, the more faith you are walking in, and the bigger the story will be of what God has done. Don't look at "you can't do that" as a negative input – say thank you and keep on looking to God, because it's true: without Him, it is impossible. But with Him, all things are possible (Matthew 19:26).

> ***Now faith is confidence in what we hope for and assurance about what we do not see. (Hebrews 11:1)***

When we're looking at our circumstances, the things that we see have the power to completely cloud our vision. But here, faith is an assurance in what we do not see: it's choosing to put the truth, which may not be seen, over what we see in our circumstances.

This verse highlights the two "kinds" of faith which we are required to exercise: the first is believing that I am created, that everything that the Word says about my identity in Christ is true; and the second is believing that God can do all things, that He is my healer and provider, and that I have every blessing in Him.

The first is about confidence in God and who He is – this comes from hearing the Word, from a first-hand relationship with God, and from this experiential knowledge of Christ. But faith that God can do all things requires **confidence in what we hope for**: it means trusting that He is working, that He is doing and will do great things. It means looking beyond what we see in our circumstances and having **assurance in what we do not see:** the second is an assurance that God can do all that He has promised that He will do.

Faith is putting the truth of God over the our perception of reality, and choosing to believe the truth – having an assurance of what we do not see – over the present reality that we see around us. It is to keep going back to God and His Word for the truth, instead of letting our faith be shaken by our circumstances. We do not need to be defined by what we see in our story so far: in faith we can look to the truth of who God says we are as a new creation.

I Am Good Enough

Fear of failure can keep us in bondage and stop us from going after the things that God has called us to do; we feel like we're not good enough, not qualified – and what if we mess it up? We would have disappointed God, we would have wasted a time and effort, and we'd look like a failure to everyone else. People might question if God actually asked us to do that thing; maybe we should just stick to what we were doing before.

Not knowing how something will turn out can be the scariest thing. But this is where God is calling us to have faith: faith that does not come from our own works and the success that we have in our own eyes, but from the Faithful One. When we're transformed by a radical relationship with Jesus, and compelled by His love, we don't live for ourselves anymore. We don't live just to live up to the expectations of others. We don't try to please God out of a need to be right with Him by law; but we live in the truth that we are pure in front of Him, because of Jesus.

When we are new creations, and have Christ in us, we are not working out our own mission, but God's mission. We've given up our own ambitions, our own ego, and we're not going after success in our own eyes, but success in His. Let this take the pressure off a bit: you are successful, simply because you have Christ in you, and because He is working through you. You are good enough, because your identity is in being a child of God, and living not in your own power, but in His.

This is what we are told to do, in Christ:

Set your mind on things above, not on earthly things. (Colossians 3:2)

When we look at God, we take our eyes off ourselves, and instead of seeing things from our perspective, we see things from His. Faith means taking your eyes off yourself and your circumstances, and looking at what Jesus has done for you. When Jesus died, He took all of our failure, all of our fear, our uncertainty, our mistakes and the times when we don't match up. Because of Him, nothing is even on us; it doesn't depend on us, or even on how much faith we feel we have. Faith is not a currency that we exchange for good things; faith is ***"confidence in what we hope for and assurance about what we do not see." (Hebrews 11:1)*** The uncertainty and fear that we can feel when our circumstances don't seem great **is not the truth**. Fear comes when we look around us at the things that we can see; but faith is assurance in what we do not see. Fear and uncertainty can't be from God, because He doesn't give us a spirit of fear, but of ***"power, and of love, and of a sound mind." (2 Timothy 1:7, KJV[2])***

If we have our mind on God and heavenly things, and not on earthly things, then faith becomes the lens that we view everything through; it means that we can stop focusing on our worry, stress, our own ability and the things that we lack, because all we see is Him.

Notice that it says to set your **mind**, not your eyes, on heavenly things. It doesn't mean glancing up every occasionally, but in living with our mind firmly in heaven with Him. We're asked to take our mind **completely off** earthly things – not keep a foot in each camp so we can go back to worry when things really heat up. This seems so impossible – but here's how it is possible for us to do this:

For you died, and your life is now hidden with Christ in God. When Christ, who is your life, appears, then you also will appear with him in glory. (Colossians 3:3-4)

When you accepted your salvation, the old you **died**; it is completely gone, and now your life is hidden in Him. In faith, we can look around and

---

[2] King James Version

only see things of heaven; and when we're living with our mind in this place, the things of the world really don't matter anymore.

As a child, our favourite place to go away on holiday was a small holiday cottage in Devon, on the south coast of the UK. I don't remember much about this place, but one thing that sticks in my mind is the cupboard under the stairs; the perfect little cubby-hole for my brother and I to play in. This cupboard seemed like the biggest place in the world; there were so many dark corners and a ceiling that I couldn't touch, even standing on my tiptoes, and it made the perfect place to go exploring. There was something that felt very safe about this cupboard – it was warm, and comfortable, and when the door was closed nothing else mattered; I could only see the place that I was in.

This is the same safety and security that we have when our minds are in Christ. There are things that go on in the world; there are circumstances that might try to throw us, but there's a protection in being completely hidden and covered. When we are saved, our life becomes the life of Christ, and we are completely covered by Him.

Put to death, therefore, whatever belongs to your earthly nature: sexual immorality, impurity, lust, evil desires and greed, which is idolatry. (Colossians 3:5)

This is not about behaving in the right way so that we will be acceptable to God; our behaviour has no effect on the love that God has for us, because all He sees is Jesus as we are covered by Him. Instead, the way that we choose to live, and the decisions that we make come from a place of deciding whether we will participate in life, or death. These things do not bring life, they bring death. They belong to death with our old selves, and as new creations we have the power to send them there, rather than bringing them into our lives as new creations.

These are things that put us in the position that God should be in our lives; idolatry is seeing ourselves, or other things, as in a higher position than God – ultimately letting these things be Lord of our lives. They are things that we take part in when we do not know any better; but when we know God, we have a choice in what we make of Lord of our lives.

You used to walk in these ways, in the life you once lived. But now you must also rid yourselves of all things such things as these: anger, rage, malice, slander, and filthy language from your lips. (Colossians 3:7-8)

Our old selves are gone and the new creation is here. As long as we keep taking part in these things, we are trying to live as the old self, trying to resurrect it from the dead, rather than living hidden in Him. This is not about behaviour, but freedom; we are not the old self trying to be a better person, but a completely new creation – and the things that bring death have no power in our lives.

Do not lie to each other, since you have taken off your old self with its practices and have put on the new self, which is being renewed in knowledge in the image of its Creator. (Colossians 3:9-10)

Just as we are a new creation, so is everybody else who knows Christ as their Lord: they are new creations, and have taken off the old self. So, when we look at each other, and we only see the things of the old creation and encourage them to stay in that place by making the assumption that that is all they are, we are lying to them; instead, they are a new creation, covered by Christ, just as we are. Instead of letting their behaviour be the box that we put them in, we can call them out into their real identity, bigger than we could imagine. We do not need to be like the rest of the world, who label people by the way that they look and act, but we can choose to look past them, and call them out into who they really are.

When we are born again in Christ, we **take off** our old self. Like a coat, if it is taken off, it is not on us at all anymore – we are free from it! And like a coat, when we put on the new self, we are surrounded by it, it covers all that is underneath, and there is nothing to add to it. Although it is whole, just as it is when we put it on, it is constantly being **renewed** in the image of God. Being born again is just the beginning of a glorious story: constantly transforming into the image of Christ. It is not our behaviour that is renewed, but our knowledge of God: instead of life being a self-improvement course, we enter into a promise, like a marriage, and then spend the rest of our life getting to know our Creator.

<u>The Disciples</u>

In the Gospels, we read about the disciples – twelve people that Jesus took from their normal lives, their ordinary situations, and invited them on an adventure with Him. These people weren't anything special – they were fishermen, the lowest of the low in their culture. In that society, the Jews knew that the Scriptures had authority over their lives: they didn't know God, but their behaviour was based on the Scriptures. To live what they believed was a righteous life, Jewish men would seek out a rabbi or a teacher and ask if they could be trained by them, following them and totally submitting to their authority in every area of their lives.

But Jesus did something radical. He invited people to walk with Him; people who wouldn't have considered themselves worthy to walk with a rabbi. He showed them that righteousness was not found in the way that they behaved, but in their salvation. Throughout the gospels, we read of the ways that Jesus taught His disciples; letting them have experiences, and stretching their faith and trust in God through these. He came to the disciples when they had this fear of failure, and instead of reinforcing their belief that they couldn't do it, He helped them to trust:

When they had rowed about three or four miles, they saw Jesus approaching the boat, walking on water; and they were frightened. But he said to them, "It is I; don't be afraid." Then they were willing to take him into the boat, and immediately the boat reached the shore where they were heading. (John 6:19-21)

When we've got a spirit of fear, it's like we're in the boat on our own, not sure where we're going, unable to see the shore. And like the disciples, when we see Jesus heading towards us, we can recognise Him, even when fear is still gripping us. It takes Jesus to speak to break the fear of man, the fear of failure – and then, when we've got Jesus in the boat with us, He gets us where we're going. When Jesus got into the boat with the disciples, He didn't necessarily change the direction of the boat: He worked with the disciples, and moved them in the direction that they were heading anyway.

Know this: Jesus loves you, Jesus accepts you. I pray that this revelation will really sink into your heart; because if we really know the acceptance of Christ, how can we feel rejected? Faith means putting the truth of our acceptance by Christ over our circumstances, when we might feel like we're out in the boat on our own. Jesus is speaking to you – all you need is to accept Him and hear His voice. Instead of a spirit of fear, God has given us a spirit of love and sound mind: what if instead of living in this spirit of fear, we live with a spirit of faith? If we are conscious of what the enemies' power is, and if we feel like he can overcome us, we will always see the difficulties in our circumstances; but we can look at who God is, and know that His power is in us. Instead of looking at the difficult situations as something that can overcome us, we can look at them as an opportunity to feed our faith. With a spirit of faith, I believe and I speak – not *if* I see, *then* I speak.

You have an invitation from God: to walk with Him, and to go on this great adventure with Him; you are chosen not because of who you are, but because of who He is.

Questions for Reflection

1. *Was there anything in Pete's story that inspired you?*
2. *Whose story is inspiring or encouraging to you in your own life?*
3. *What part of your life is your "faith gap" in?*
4. *What Biblical truth/verse can you choose to stand on for that faith gap?*

CHAPTER THREE
I AM LOVED

"Whenever I get gloomy with the state of the world, I think about the arrivals gate at Heathrow Airport. General opinion is starting to make out that we live in a world of hatred and greed, but I don't see that. It seems to me that love is everywhere. Often, it's not particularly dignified or newsworthy, but it's always there - fathers and sons, mothers and daughters, husbands and wives, boyfriends, girlfriends, old friends. When the planes hit the Twin Towers, as far as I know, none of the phone calls from the people on board were messages of hate or revenge - they were all messages of love. If you look for it, I've got a sneaky feeling you'll find that love actually is all around."

- **Hugh Grant, Love Actually**

You only need to look around for a little while in our culture to be blasted with a picture of what we think love is. Rom-Coms, hearts and teddy bears, sex, lust, 50 shades of whatever. Feeling like we are loved can be dependent on whether our life matches up to this image of what our culture says that love is: and if our relationships don't look like a rom-com, we can feel like we don't match up – like we're not good enough. But to know what love really is, we only need to look to God – the one who loves us more than we can comprehend, who created us, who loves because He is love. The Bible sings of the extent of His love:

For God so loved the world that he gave his one and only Son, that whoever believes in him shall not perish but have eternal life. (John 3:16)

This is the truth - it doesn't say that God loved the world a little bit, or that God could have loved the world if only we hadn't screwed up so much: it says that God **so** loves the world. God experienced love so much, that He needed to send His son to redeem the world, that He might know us as His sons and daughters. God is chasing after you, He's pursuing you with this love that is greater than you imagine – and yet we look away from this love, and instead look at the portrayal of love that is all around us.

Our God is a loving God, and He stretches His net wide – He says that ***whoever believes in Him*** will have eternal life – that's all it takes. God is not looking for the best of the best - He's looking for people who love Him, who will give Him their lives and trust Him to do His best in them. And Jesus was not **Plan B** – He wasn't something that God had to scramble together because we messed up the plan. He's an awesome God, and He knew exactly what was going to play out, and what we needed to be able to live in His goodness – Jesus is God chasing after His creation, from the very beginning.

When we begin to get hold of the extent of the love that God has for us, it radically changes the way that we live. There was a video that went viral on social media this year – a news reporter, presenting a report via Skype from his own home, looking very important with a suit and a tie, talking about South Korea – when in bursts daughter Marion, age four, closely followed by baby brother James, in his walker. A few seconds delay, and then in comes a very flustered Mum, who drags them both out and closes the door behind them. If you haven't seen the clip, I highly recommend looking it up – search for "children interrupt BBC news interview" for the best forty-five seconds of your day. My favourite thing about the clip is the absolute swagger and confidence that the daughter walks into the room with: this is my Dad's office, and I am his daughter. What could he possibly be doing that is more important? Why would he not want to see me right now?! She walks straight in, evidently comfortable around her Dad and being in her Dad's space – why would she not be able to go to him?

The unending love that God has for us means that we get to go to Him with the same confidence and swagger as the little girl approaches her father with. There is absolutely no reason why our Father would not want to spend time with us – we are the most important thing in the world to Him. What could He possibly be doing that is more important?!

Living loved, or living to be loved?

Chances are that the idea that you are unique, brilliant, gorgeous, or fabulous isn't a message that is new to you. We know that we should know our worth; we should be confident, and we shouldn't have to deal with self-esteem issues. Bruno Mars sings it at us: ***because you're amazing, just the way you are.*** We watch movies of the protagonist realising who they are: they can overcome the challenge, they can go to the dance, they can do what their heart desires – because they are worth it.

But if we only know we're amazing because Bruno Mars says we are, that's going to be shattered easily by whatever the next person says we are. It's great to know your worth, in our culture, as long as it stays convenient; as long as in the end, we remember our place. As long as our self-worth only really takes us to a place where we fit in with everyone else – we can be a nice person, have a lot of friends, and live quite happily in that place.

But what if our self-worth doesn't come from what other people say about us, or how we think we should feel about ourselves, but from knowing not just *who* we are, but *whose* we are? There's a difference: suddenly this isn't static, it isn't just about self-confidence. This kind of self-worth – knowing that we are valuable because we are created, redeemed, and known by God – leads to such a full life. Jesus said that He came so that we might have life, and have it to the full. Believing that I'm great is twee and nice; but, in my experience, a relationship with the God who made me leads to adventure, joy, peace beyond measure. It means that it doesn't actually matter what the world says about me, because my Dad thinks the world of me.

Let's look again at the story of Abraham in the Bible. At the beginning of his story, his life didn't look like much at all: he didn't have any kids, he was old; and to him, that looked like God had forgotten him, like he didn't matter. He talked about this with God, and this is what God said to Abraham: **"Look up at the heavens and count the stars – if indeed you can count them. So shall your offspring be." (Genesis 15:5)**

The amazing thing is that Abraham chose to believe that what God said about him was true; and because of this, he lived out the future that God had for him. He's called righteous for this – not because of what he did, or how he lived, but because he chose to believe that what God said about him was true.

I wonder: at this moment, are you living in the knowledge that you are loved by God, or are you living your life trying to earn love – God's, or other people's? We can spend our whole life trying to earn God's approval – if I pray a certain way, go to church enough, do all the right things, treat people in the right way, then I'll be right with God – but this is exhausting! This is religion – robbing us of our unique identity in exchange for conformity with this system that only looks good on the outside. On the inside, we're burnt out, tired, fed up with God. But as we've talked about – we don't need to do this! God is delighted in us because we are His sons and daughters – He has already done everything that needs to be done on the cross.

When you're in a relationship, you don't date for ninety years with the hope of maybe, someday, knowing each other well enough to get married; you get married, and then with this promise tying you together, you spend the rest of your lives on an adventure together. This is so much like our relationship with God: we don't need to spend our whole life striving, constantly having to live up to God's standards: God has made the promise, He says that we are loved, that we are redeemed, and that we are walking with Him – and we get to live in this love.

Like an Apple Tree Among the Trees of the Forest

One of my favourite books in the Bible is a book called Song of Solomon, also known as the Song of Songs. It holds verses of songs; the kind of songs that, in the tradition of the Jewish people at the time, would have been sung throughout a wedding ceremony. They describe the whole process of meeting and falling in love with a partner, from first catching sight, to the wedding and the consummation, to looking forward to life together. The beautiful text switches between words from **Him**, and words from **Her**, with **Him** being the husband in the wedding ceremony, potentially written with the image of a king like King Solomon in mind, and **Her** being the bride. But we can also read the book as a conversation between Christ, the bridegroom, and the bride, the Church – that's you and me. It's a great place to find out all about the relationship that we get to have with Jesus, and to hear exactly how He feels about you.

We find these beautiful words from the bride, describing her bridegroom:

> ***Like an apple tree among the trees of the forest is my beloved among the young men. I delight to sit in his shade, and his fruit is sweet to my taste. Let him lead me to the banquet hall, and let his banner over me be love. (Song of Songs 2:3-4)***

This is who our Saviour is: He is like an apple tree among the trees of the forest, a person of rare, precious beauty among a crowd of normality and sameness. Apple trees serve a purpose and produce beautiful fruit, while the trees of the forest are simply there to be a part of the crowd. His shade brings us rest and is delightful to sit in, and His fruit – the things that He produces – is so sweet to us.

He is waving a banner over you of love – love is all that He is shouting over you, because He is so proud of you, and His love for you is so pure. Jesus is cuckoo about you! The song goes on to sing of the things that Jesus is asking of you:

> ***My beloved spoke and said to me, "Arise my darling, my beautiful one, come with me"… "Show me your face, let me hear your voice; for your voice is sweet and your face is lovely" (Song of Songs 2:10, 14)***

Let those words soak into your soul for a moment – **Arise, my darling, and come with me**. In His gentleness, Jesus is calling us to get up and go with Him, hand in hand, because we know Him and love Him and trust Him so fully. And when we choose to do that, He leads us so gently; just the two of us on an adventure. He asks us to show Him our face and let Him hear our voice with boldness, knowing that He loves to hear us, and that our face is beautiful to Him. Whatever else you put on yourself, however you feel about yourself, know this, precious one: He thinks your face is lovely, and He loves to hear your voice. He is completely, head over heels, totally in love with you and spending time with you is His favourite thing to do.

These songs speak of the wonderful love of God, who loves you with this unending love because you are worth loving. But hear this if you are single: it is absolutely acceptable for us to expect to be able to speak these words over our future husbands and wives too – that they are like apricot trees among trees of the forest, with delightful shade and fruit sweet to taste. You are pretty crazy special, and you are worth so much to Jesus, so any future partner is going to have to be pretty crazy special to break into that – and that's okay. That's the way that it's supposed to be, because you are worth being loved by someone pretty crazy special – an apricot tree among the trees of the forest. I pray that you will recognise them by how special they are. I pray that sitting with them will bring you so much delight, and that the fruit they produce will be so sweet to your taste. I pray that they will match up to Jesus' standards – not perfect, but righteous.

On Relationships (and Singletons)

It's near impossible to think around the topic of love without your brain wandering on to the topic of relationships, or lack thereof. There are so many Christian books about dating out there that I don't have much to add to the conversation. In my years of youth pastoring, I've sat at the back of the hall during many a talk on Christian dating, Christian relationships, marriage and boundaries; but not a single one on singleness. All the while, churches are full of single young people: most of whom are too terrified to talk to each other, because they don't know where to start.

As Christians, single or not, it is key to start from a place of knowing how loved you are – before you are loved by a significant other. Our identity is found in being rooted and grounded in the love of Christ, not the love of other people. When this is the case, our relationships stop being about the need for affection and approval from another in order to feel fulfilled, and become about going on a crazy adventure with a partner, both running at full speed towards Christ. That, my dear friend, is worth waiting for, and it is totally OK if this is not found in the first person to show interest in dating you. Know that you are valuable, just as you are; get comfortable in your own skin, and know that God has got your back in this.

When you talk to Christians about being single, there are various responses. Some will tilt their head to the side, give you a gentle smile, and say something like "it's OK, he's out there somewhere". Some of those who are married will nod knowingly and talk about how much they admire you, and how much time you have to do the things that they can't. And some will invite themselves over, bring you chocolate ice cream, and talk into the night about dream guys and hypothetical situations. They're my favourite, and not just because of the chocolate ice cream.

There's an incredible woman called Neith Boyce, who wrote a column for Vogue in 1898 called the Bachelor Girl, celebrating single life in a culture where marriage was the norm. *"I shall never be an old maid, because I have elected to be a Girl Bachelor"* she writes: trying to show a generation that she was possible – that marriage is a choice, not a default. *"There were always enough who wanted to get married and carry on the race… If a woman liked to play with words and set them in patterns and make pictures with them, and was taking care of herself and bothering nobody, and enjoyed her life without a lot of bawling children around, why shouldn't she?"* writes Boyce, in the **1890s**. She was trying to convince the world that she was possible, in a world that said that life was impossible without a husband; I'm not sure things have changed all that much.

The sad thing is, I'm not sure that column would be published in a glossy magazine in our current culture. A culture where the phrase "the single woman" is only on a cover when followed with the words "… and our tips for finding the dream man", or "and why a one-night-stand might be great for you". A culture where, if you're single, you're often seen as 'waiting' – *"why don't you just get out there and meet someone?"; "Ooh, I've got a friend who would be perfect for you".* Or we're praised for 'holding out', keeping ourselves from that thing that we obviously want so badly.

The idea that someone was writing a column in the 1890s about how **my** life is possible is amazing to me; while I'm having the same conversations every day – No, I'm not lonely all the time. No, there's nothing wrong with me. No, I don't want to go on a random date with your random mate Dave from accounts; I'm doing just great by myself, thank you very much.

A (single) friend of mine was once talking to a long-term singleton, who looked at her, gave her the gentle smile, and said: "So how do you do it?

How do you have the strength to do this on your own every day, without drowning in loneliness?" Now this friend is one of the most beautiful, strong, wonderful people I know, and she's rocking life on her own. So she looked at her friend, smiled and said "I get up. I live a day. And then I go to bed. There's no secret". She's not living life as a single person – she's just living life. And she's not waiting for something to happen to her. It's not that she doesn't want to get married. It's not that she doesn't want to be with someone, to love someone. But she isn't shaping her life around waiting to get married. Instead, she's getting on with everything that she can do on her own – and she's owning it. She's out there, changing lives, changing the world... without a husband. Instead of putting her purpose on hold, she's getting on with it, and she inspires me every day.

One phrase we Christians throw around a lot is "our hearts' desires". Those things that we want with all our heart, that shape the way that we spend our days. And for us singletons, it's kind of assumed that marriage is top of that list. And it might be – but there are so many hopes and dreams in there. I would love to be married. I'd love to change the world with my partner. But there's so much more. I want to be a Mum. I want to inspire people, to encourage others. I want to see people come out of the darkness and in to the light. I want to travel, to learn, to know more and more about this beautiful world. I want to learn languages and experience cultures that are different to mine. I want to love God with all my heart, all my soul, all my mind and all my strength. And that stuff is so much more important to me than being a wife.

Things to Remember:

You Are a Work in Progress:

The way that you live your life is so important – it's all about the here and now. As Christians we look forward to heaven, but God is interested in the process of you becoming everything that He made you to be. God is not preoccupied with whether you are going to find a boyfriend or a girlfriend. What He cares about is you – whether you are living in everything that He created for you. Salvation is just as much about what God is doing in your life today as where we go when we die.

So focus on being the best version of you that you can be. When you do that, you will inspire people, you will encourage people, and you will achieve more than you can possibly imagine. And guess what – that is so attractive. Living in everything that you have called to be makes you so beautiful.

God has a Purpose for Your Life:

Do not underestimate the reason that you are here, by instead living to simply be the other half of somebody else. You were put here on purpose, for a purpose, and you are needed here. Those people that look at you and talk about how much time you have to do all the things that they can't because they're married – they're right. You can commit your life to loving God and loving people – and there's no-one else that you need to consider in that decision.

There has been so much that I've been able to be a part of in this life that I would not have been involved in if I was focused on spending time with my other half every night. I've been able to say "yes" to the late nights, the long days, and the trips all over the place, because I'm the only person involved in those decisions.

I think the best relationships are not where one person leans on the other and takes on their purpose, but where both are absolutely, 100% going for it – together. And that's worth waiting for. Don't throw that away for what looks attractive right now.

God is Able:

Of all the areas of my life, this is the one that I am most likely to try and take into my own hands. "This just doesn't seem to be happening. But if I just log on to this site…" But God doesn't need our help. When we trust in God, we can give up the need to try and sort it all out ourselves. We don't need to take the wheel, we can find joy, peace and contentment, just where we are. We can trust that God sees our hearts' desires, that He knows us, and loves us, and wants the best for us. And we can believe that He's got it handled, and enjoy the journey.

There is absolutely nothing wrong with wanting to be married – God LOVES marriage, and He designed us for these kinds of relationships. But do not make the search for this partner to be about looking for love, when we have a Father who wants to lavish you with more love than any human can give you.

Rooted in Love

And I pray that you, being rooted and established in love, may have power, together with all the Lord's holy people, to grasp how wide and long and

high and deep is the love of Christ, and to know this love that surpasses knowledge – that you may be filled to the measure of all the fullness of God. (Ephesians 3:17-19)

There are many things in life that I do not understand, but there are many things in life that I do not need to fully understand to be able to use. I don't understand the inner workings of how electricity works, but I can flick a switch. I may have a lot of questions about God and life and things that happen and do not happen; but I can know that I am a child of God, I can ask God for this love, and I can grasp how wide and long and high and deep this love is – not because I understand everything, but because I know who my God is. This love surpasses knowledge – it's not something we can rationalise and fit into our box, because His love is beyond understanding. This is an incredible thing – it means that God loving me is not dependant on my understanding of God's love. Instead, He fills me to the measure with His love, for free, and I can be rooted and established in His love, and live out of this place.

When I'm rooted and established in His love, my power is not found in all the things that I "should" do to earn His love; in going to church, and praying in the right way, and loving people enough. Instead, I have the power to just live in this love – to run head first into the difficult situations, to show His love to the people who are hardest to love, to walk through the storms, to do the things that He is calling me to – not because I'm able, but because He is able. I'm so full of His love that no matter what He asks me to do, I can do it.

The Epic Love Story

This love that God has for us is so much more than fuzzy feelings and being comfortable. In God's love, we are called into a story that is much bigger than our own:

I became a servant of this gospel by the gift of God's grace given me through the working of his power. Although I am less than the least of all the Lord's people, this grace was given me: to preach to the Gentiles the boundless riches of Christ. (Ephesians 3:7-8)

Note that this does not say that I'm a servant to the church, or a slave to anything – but a servant of the gospel. Our primary calling, our main job in life, is to be a part of His story, through His wonderful grace that He has given to us so freely. It was given to us through the working of His power, and this power lives now in us; as it is not us who live, but Him. In Christ, there's no position or power that is our own: I'm now dead to myself, and alive in Him. Although I'm the least of all of God's people, God doesn't regard me like this; He wants all of His children to live in this power. No rank, no job title, no person is over anybody else. Our purpose does not come from the position that we're put in by human efforts, or the title that is given us, but from our identity and our security in Him.

And to make plain to everyone the administration of this mystery, which for ages past was kept hidden in God, who created all things. (Ephesians 3:9)

There were things that were not available to us, that were kept separated from us; curtains separated God's love from the rest of the world, priests were the worlds' link between God and the people. But because of what Jesus did on the cross, we have complete, unlimited access to God. In the moment that Jesus died on the cross, the curtain in the temple was ripped from top to bottom – note, not from bottom to top – ending the separation between God and His people; a symbol of the old dying to itself, and the new promise coming in. When that curtain was ripped, the Spirit of God left that temple, never again to live in a place built by human hands – free to anyone who asked for it, and we were freed from the religious system, from the law and the boundaries that kept people from knowing God;

Because of Jesus, the mysteries of God are no longer mysteries to us. We can have access to all of this in Christ; and our job, as sons and daughters of God, is to make plain to everyone the things of God, which are open and free to them, too.

His intent was that now, through the church, the manifold wisdom of God should be made known to the rulers and authorities in the heavenly realms, according to His eternal purpose that he accomplished in Christ Jesus our Lord. (Ephesians 3:10-11)

The wisdom of God can only be learnt through revelation – through direct relationship with God, our Father. The curtain in the temple was a constant reminder that because of our sin, we all are unfit for the presence of God; but because of Jesus, He promises His presence is always with us – sin is not powerful enough to break this promise. God's intent is that now, through the Church, this presence and wisdom is made known to all, through an intimate relationship with God. This is His eternal purpose, which He has accomplished in Christ – it's been done; it's up to us to accept all that He has done for us and to walk in this salvation.

All that God achieved through Christ Jesus; all of the incredible things that He has done to free us, and to live in us, was because of this great love that God has for His people. You are part of one awesome, epic, amazing love story; the best love story that has ever been written. From the days of the people of Israel turning away from Him, God has been chasing after His people, tirelessly pursuing us. Jesus died so that He might have a relationship with His children. He's there – all it takes is a "yes".

This is the truth; that we are loved by the God who created us. He is pursuing a relationship with you; even if you were the only person left on the earth, He still would have sent His son to die for you so that He might have a relationship with you, His child, whom He loves and with whom He is well pleased.

<u>The Original Love Story – God's Love for Israel</u>

The whole story of the Israelites is a love story between God and His people. In the Psalms, we read about what He does for those that He loves:

The Lord builds up Jerusalem; he gathers the exiles of Israel. He heals the brokenhearted and binds up their wounds. He determines the number of stars and calls them each by name. (Psalm 147:2-4)

This God is the God who spoke the stars in the sky into existence with a word, and knows the exact number of them; and yet He sees those who are brokenhearted, and bends down to heal them and bind up their wounds. **He** does it. The psalm does not say that He expects the Israelites to sort themselves out and worship Him - He does it, without any expectation of love in return. He does it simply because they are His children and He loves them. Let's not doubt that He who knows the number of stars in the sky, and grains of sand on the shore, knows us in just as much detail and cares for us so much more.

In our darkest moments, when everything seems to tumble and fall around us, in the moments when we feel the most alone, God is there with us: His heart is for those who are brokenhearted. He's crouched down next to you on the floor, ready to wipe every tear from your eyes, pick up the pieces and help you carry on. He's so much bigger than whatever it was that put you there, and He's strong enough to carry you out of it.

His pleasure is not in the strength of the horse, nor his delight in the legs of the warrior; the Lord delights in those who fear him, who put their hope in his unfailing love. (Psalm 147:10-11)

I love this truth that we find in the psalms. God is not interested in the might of an army, or our physical strength, or what we can do; instead, He

delights in those who hope in His unfailing love. Therefore, His love **is** unfailing and God loves those who hope in it – there's nothing that is big or ugly enough for God's love to fail us, and there's nothing that we can do that is bad enough for Him to take this love from us. God fights for us and He does not depend on our strength or our armies or how much we can look after ourselves - He wants to give us His protection, His assistance, His strength. His love is unfailing; but hope is a choice from our end.

God begins His relationship with Israel like the relationship between a parent and a child: ***"I have reared children and brought them up, but they have rebelled against me. The ox knows its master, the donkey its owners' manger, but Israel does not know, my people do not understand." (Isaiah 1:2-3)***

Parents will try to raise their child to share in their values and the ways that they live; but, ultimately the child is free to make their own decisions about whose rule they will live under. Israel, like children, decided to turn away from God and rebel against Him - and, just like an earthly father, God was jealous for His people.

When this happens, the child, although they feel free, is afflicted: they would be better with the parents' guidance, and they suffer by trying to go their own way. We read about the effect that this choice has on the people:

Your whole head is injured, your whole heart afflicted. From the sole of your foot to the top of your head there is no soundness – only wounds and welts and open sores, not cleansed or bandaged or soothed with olive oil. (Isaiah 1:5-6)

The writer was speaking to a group of people who were used to beating as a common punishment. They knew what it was like to be injured, but they would have soothed their wounds. They understood what it would be like to go through this kind of pain and not be able to soothe your wounds: this, they heard, is what it was like for them to turn away from God.

But, God loved His people, and He did not leave them in that place: ***"Come now, let us settle the matter," says the Lord. "Though your sins are like scarlet, they shall be as white as snow; though they are red as crimson, they shall be like wool." (Isaiah 1:18)*** God wanted His people to return to Him; He wanted them to lean on Him and look to Him for redemption. When they would, God promised, their sins that were red like scarlet would be washed white as snow; he would not see their sin and shame, but their faith and purity. Because of Jesus, this is what happens for us; we look to God, we accept our salvation, and our loving Father does not see us as red like scarlet, but as white as snow.

I love how everything in the Old Testament points to Jesus, like signposts. In Isaiah 4, we read about what's coming for the people of God: ***"In that day the branch of the Lord will be beautiful and glorious, and the fruit of the land will be the pride and glory of the survivors in Israel." (Isaiah 4:2)*** God is promising his people a hope and a future; and what's the branch of the Lord? Jesus! The New Testament talks a lot about Jesus being a branch - and here He is, thousands of years before He turned up on earth. Out of the remnant of God's people, a branch would grow. He would bless the world and bring peace to the mess; Jesus!

When we're in a mess, when we've turned away from God and tried to do things our own way, God takes the ruins and brings beauty. Out of the ashes rises hope, and a future for those who trust in Him. We can take refuge in Him, we can make Him our hiding place, because He wants to protect us and bring us hope.

Surely the rising of the mighty waters will not reach them. You are my hiding place; you will protect me from trouble and surround me with songs of deliverance. (Psalm 32:6-7)

I've spent some time recently with a gorgeous baby boy called Jeremiah, and his Mum, Bryony. I watched the two at a wedding yesterday; Jeremiah is so tiny, and although he has a habit of running around and causing trouble, when he's around, everyone stops and cares for him. Jeremiah's Dad must seem like a giant to him, and I love the look on his face as his Dad bends down to pick him up; there's so much awe and wonder in his eyes. This is how God's people should be looking up at God: full of awe and wonder as God bends down with tender love and kindness. While the world around us can be shaky and scary at times, we have a loving Father who not only rules over everything, but sees us and treats us with kindness, as His children.

He is as big as the giant of a Dad seems to a baby: when the mighty waters rise and everything seems to pile up against us, they will never reach the heights of our Father, who protects us with this kindness. We can hide in this protection, knowing that He has promised to protect us from trouble, and that He's ready to swoop us up in his arms at any moment.

Love is

We can spend our whole lives looking for love. But if we live knowing that we are loved by God, instead of living looking for God, it's a much quicker search: God's love is so free and available to us that we don't need to do anything to get it.

Love is patient, love is kind. It does not envy, it does not boast, it is not proud. It does not dishonour others, it is not self-seeking, it is not easily angered, it keeps no record of wrongs. Love does not delight in evil but rejoices with the truth. It always protects, always trusts, always hopes, always perseveres. Love never fails. (1 Corinthians 13:4-8)

You've probably heard these verses before – they're read at every wedding, thinking about the characteristics that are good to have in a marriage. They're pretty great characteristics to have – patience, kindness… – and most people will try to go through life trying to display these things as much as possible; it's generally accepted that they make you a nice person.

And in 1 John, this verse comes up, *"Dear friends, let us love one another, for love comes from God. Everyone who loves has been born of God and knows God. Whoever does not know love does not know God, because God is love." (1 John 4:7-8)*

God is love. That doesn't mean that God is loving, or that God loves – He is love. Everything about Him is love; which means that this idea that we might have of God as some far-off guy, floating on a cloud, being angry at us, doesn't really work out.

If God is love, then all of these things are integral to the nature of God – *God is patient, God is kind. He does not envy, He does not boast, He is not proud. He does not dishonour others, He is not self-seeking, He is not easily angered, He keeps no record of wrongs. God does not delight in evil but rejoices with the truth. He always protects, always trusts, always hopes, always perseveres. God never fails.*

So if we have an image of God as anything other than these things, there's something that we're seriously missing about His nature. If you see God as angry at you when you mess up, then there's something that you haven't quite got right: God is not easily angered. If you feel guilty and ashamed of the things that you have done, as though God is holding these things over you, then you're not living in His freedom: God keeps no record of wrongs; He doesn't see the worst in us, He seems the best in us, and that is all He sees. If we feel like we're alone or that God has given up on us, then we're missing out: God never fails. He always protects, always trusts, always hopes, always perseveres. That doesn't sound like a God that would give up on His kids.

His word says, *"**We love, because He first loved us.**" (1 John 4:19)*

We can only love because He first loved us; therefore, when we are loving people, we're not loving them with our love – we're loving them with His love. Let this take the weight off a little bit – it's OK to recognise that it is difficult to love some people, because we're not asked to love them in our own strength, but with the love that He has given us.

We have all of these things, not because of how amazing and loving we are, but because we have God living in us – we died, and now He lives through us. When we're interacting with other people, it's not our love, it's His.

In Him – "*I am patient, I am kind. I do not envy, I do not boast, I am not proud. I do not dishonour others, I am not self-seeking, I am not easily angered, I keep no record of wrongs. I do not delight in evil but rejoice with the truth. I always protect, always trust, always hopes, always persevere. In Him, I never fail*".

We can't wrap ourselves in bubble wrap and never experience any hurt or pain; but we can choose to look to the God who loves us. Hear this: God is chasing after you. He's on your side. The storms will come, people will hurt you, things will happen that our outside of your control, but God has this love for you that is bigger than all of that; and if you call to Him, He will hear your plea. You are so ridiculously, crazily, inexplicably loved by the God who made you, and He's waiting for you with open arms, to run in to Him.

Questions for Reflection:

1. *Check your current heart position: are you living loved, or living to be loved?*

2. *Was there a part of the love story of Israel that stood out to you?*

3. *Which Biblical truth are you going to choose to stand in in this area?*

CHAPTER FOUR
I AM ATTRACTIVE

It's funny, and yet not surprising, that the way we look, and the way that others look, is one of the most important factors in our lives. We spend hours trying to make ourselves look acceptable before we go out. We dress in a certain way, do our hair in a certain way, look a certain way, to look like the person that we want to convince the world that we are. Often, we find friends to hang out with that look like us, or we change the way that we look to look like them. It's one of the first things that you notice about a person, and people can be so harshly judged based on the way that they look.

When someone takes a photo of you and your friends, what's the first thing that you look for? Yourself, right? Me too – we all do it. If everyone else in the photo looks great but I look bad, then it's a terrible photo and must never see the light of day; but if no-one else is happy with it, but I look good, then it's going up on my wall. That's part of the reason that we use social media in the way that we do, right? We take the "perfect" selfie, put it up, and then wait for the likes and comments to roll in. Because if people don't tell us that we're attractive, then where is our worth coming from?

We like selfies because we have the power to take, retake and get that perfect picture, and no-one needs to see the ones that we rejected. We take twenty different photos at different angles until we find the one that we like, and then we tweak it, adjust the lighting, put on a filter or three. We can crop it so that the square doesn't show that stray hair, or your forehead that you're convinced is too big.

I wonder how different your day would be if, in the morning, you were told that you were beautiful; not based on the way you try to look for other people, or the clothes you had picked out, but just you. I wonder how different your day would be if you believed that you were attractive, just in being you. I could tell you: "don't get so caught up in your looks, looks don't matter". But, in all honesty, I'd struggle with that, because I, like most people in the world, don't want to be repulsive. No-one wants to be ugly. Our looks are the thing that have the potential to stick out in a world that is telling us to fit in with everyone else. So we put all of our effort into not standing out, into looking acceptable, into being average; because being average and not standing out is better than people looking at you with that look on their face.

But in a world that is telling us that we are not beautiful because we do not match up to the standards that the media has set for us, it is key to find your beauty in God, who created you. In a world in which you are forever the one surrounded by slim, gorgeous friends, it is important to look to God for your acceptance and your home. In a world where we never feel like we match up and would rather be invisible, know that God hand-crafted you and put you here for a moment such as this.

Average

I really enjoy watching videos on YouTube by Dove, the cosmetics company (and I enjoy how much my job allows me to do this!). Dove produce "social experiment"-type videos, particularly focused on women and the way that we think about appearance and self-esteem. In 2015, Dove produced a video in which they had asked women to walk through one of two doors: one of which had "beautiful" written in large letters above it, and the other labelled "average". They did this all over the world, these words written in different languages; but generally, people responded in a very similar way: they walked through the "average" door.

Calling yourself beautiful feels very strange, and can feel quite arrogant. But why? At one point in the video, one of the ladies who had walked through the "average" door said this: *"Am I choosing because of what is constantly bombarded at me, and what I'm told to accept, or because of what I actually believe?"*

So much of what we choose to believe about ourselves comes from what we are told to believe, what we are bombarded with. We look at the media, at magazines, TV shows, movies, and see people who are totally out of reach. Even Instagram celebrities – these photos have been cropped, edited, photoshopped; but they're put up as if this is the norm. We compare the way we look to what is portrayed as the norm, but we're actually comparing our norm to their "best bits".

When we look in the mirror, we see all the bits that we don't like, all the bits that don't match up to the image that we think we should have. We see the bumps and the lumps, we see the proportions of our facial features that we don't think are quite right, we see the ways our clothes don't fit quite the way we would like, we see the funny things that our hair does that we've always been self-conscious of. But sit a child on your lap, and let them play with your face for a while. I've got a four-year-old friend, Vera, who, for as long as she could climb, has pulled herself up onto my knees, removed my glasses from my face, and proceeded to poke and prod, to pull my cheeks out and make them stretch. She pushes my eyebrows up until I look surprised, and then pushes them down until I look grumpy. She brushes her fingers along my lips and feels my skin. She fiddles with my earrings and plays with my earlobes.

In the eyes of a child, I am not made of lumps and bumps and horrible bits. I'm made of cheeks that stretch and skin that glows and eyebrows that can make funny expressions. I'm made of smooth lips and stretchy ears and hair that is fun to plait or tie up or play with. She doesn't look at me with any of the criticism that I look at myself with; my face brings her *pleasure*.

Many of us wish that we could trade our body out for another, but imagine for a moment, dear reader, that your face was switched for another. Imagine that one day, you woke up with Jennifer Lawrence's, or Ryan Gosling's face. Your nose replaced by theirs, your hair gone and replaced by theirs. You have your own memories, your thoughts and ideas and feelings, but their face is the one that you see in the mirror. The face that you had is gone; the stretchiness of your skin and the ears that you could tuck your hair behind and the eyes that you know so well; gone.

As much as I, like we all do, compare myself to others, and sometimes wish that I could look like another; I'm glad that I have my face. It's a face that I have got to know well over the years – all the bumps, all the scars and red bits and bits that stick out a bit. It's not perfect; but no face is. But it's a face that has been the face of my own life; it's lived as I have lived and it tells my story. I wouldn't want to replace that with another; it has been lived in, and poked and prodded and cried on and stained with make-up – but it is mine.

I Am Created

God looks at us with the same awe and curiosity as a child does when they poke and prod at our face. We were created, designed by our heavenly Father, and put here on the earth. Why? Simply, it seems, for His pleasure – He created us because He wanted to create. In Revelation, we read this:

"You are worthy, our Lord and God, to receive glory and honour and power, for you created all things, and by your will they were created and have their being." (Revelation 4:11)

We were created by His will, and that was one of the first things He did in the grand creation story. God is a creative, and therefore it gives Him pleasure to create; and, as we see right from the start, He loves to be in relationship with those that He has created.

We read how He made humans in the image and likeness of Himself: ***"So God created mankind in his own image, in the image of God he created them; male and female he created them" (Genesis 1:27);*** and because of this, humans have access into a relationship with God, and we can know and love the God who created us. We were created *in Him and for Him*, not because He needed us, but because He wanted us to know His glory and honour and power.

He is the Almighty God, the Creator, and yet He calls us friends:

You are my friends if you do what I command. I no longer call you servants, because the servant does not know his master's business. Instead, I have called you friends, for everything that I learned from my Father I have made known to you. (John 15:14-15)

He created us for His pleasure, so that we might have the pleasure of knowing Him.

Do Not Compare Your Behind the Scenes to Another's Best Bits

I love God's creation, but sometimes the business of life takes over and I'm guilty of taking it for granted. I don't spend much time in wide, open spaces. Cambridge is a very full, busy place – full of universities and students; bustling coffee shops; high streets surrounded by tall buildings. In my standard day, I go from home, to the office, and back again – I might spend some time in the town centre, or in other people's houses, or in a cafe; but it's very rare that I'm not around people and things.

First, God made light. And then he made the separation between land and sea – expanse. I find it hard to picture the earth at this point – just a wide, open space. Because we live surrounded by things, and people, and places, it's hard for us to imagine a life without them. When I live in a contained space, my ideas, thoughts and visions fit into that space. I'll only see as far as my eyes see – which is normally just in front of me. Everything becomes small to fit into my world.

But every now and then, I get out into a wide, open place, and it reminds me how big God's creation is. It reminds me that there is a bigger picture, and I begin to understand things that are beyond my own small world.

We all feel a bit overwhelmed at times. We're trying to balance workload, studying, spending time at home, spending time with friends, prioritising our health, eating right, getting enough sleep. And during those times, when life gets crazy, we make mistakes. We prioritise the wrong things. We don't get things done like we should. We curl up for a couple of hours and watch Netflix under the duvet rather than reply to that friend that is feeling neglected.

Then we look at Instagram, and Facebook, and Youtube, and we see the people who seem to be living their life so perfectly. "I bet they don't struggle with the things that I do," we think. Always looking great, always smiling, always having an exciting time. To put their life on display like that, they must be so confident, so happy with themselves, right?

Sure, some of the time. I'm sure they feel great about that snapshot of their life that they've put out for the world to see; they have no issue with the 15 minutes of their day that is on display. But here's the thing: **do not compare your Behind the Scenes, to someone else's Best Bits.**

There's an unwritten rule on Instagram at the moment, particularly among teenage girls. When you click on a profile and see just a regular teenager with hundreds or thousands of followers, it's not necessarily because they have genuine connections with all those people on a regular basis. Instead, an entire year group will follow each other, and then you follow people you do not know, in the expectation that they will follow you back, so you end up with a huge number of people who see your photos come up on their timeline. Then the expectation is that these people will engage with one another's selfies and photos, liking and commenting. Each photo that they post ends up with hundreds of likes within a day or so, with countless comments underneath**:** *"this is beautiful", "gorgeous!", "stunning <3".*

And if you've got hundreds of likes on your selfie, and people are telling you that you are beautiful, it must be true, right? Then, when someone looks at your profile, they will know that you are beautiful, because every photo has all this attention.

We all use social media to show ourselves in the best light: happy selfies with our friends, views from the mountaintops, the funniest moments of our days. What we don't all put on is the low parts, the bits that we struggle with, the moments of normality in our lives. So if we're looking at social media and comparing our regular lives to someone else's highlights, we're always going to feel small. But when we know that our identity is simply found in being a child of God, the things that other people say about us do not matter.

In my life, I've had moments of wondering if what I do really matters. Life gets crazy, things happen, and I lose sight of what I'm doing and why I'm doing it. Things can feel a bit unknown, and because of that, the world feels a bit unsafe and insecure. These are the moments when I need to return to the bigger picture: the story that I am created, that God knows me, and that I'm a part of this big world that He made. I'm reminded that I'm not here by accident; I'm not just doing things for the point of it, I'm living out a plan and a purpose that has been designed for me from the moment that God created the world. And when I'm walking in my identity in Christ, I'm reminded that it is not the praise of others that matters, whether that is praise of what my life looks like, or what my face looks like; but it is the way that God looks at me that matters. God looks at me and says *"it is good"* – He looks at me and He is pleased, and that is all that really matters.

"Do not fear, for I have redeemed you; I have summoned you by name, you are mine." (Isaiah 43:1)

The invitation that God gives us – to call on Him, and to live in relationship with Him – will lead to a life that is much bigger than you could possibly imagine. But as soon as we shrink God down to fit our world, as soon as God becomes controllable, we've lost the idea of who God is.

So here's what I've decided: **Nothing Else Really Matters.** Not the way that I look, not the things that I do, not the things that I don't think I do well enough. Not my insecurities and my fears, not the things that other people say about me; and definitely not the ways in which other people's lives seem so much bigger and better than mine. I am His, and He is mine. God created me, put me here, and I'm living my life in relationship with Him. Everything else, all the other stress that I pile on to myself – I don't need it. We don't need to be burdened, because we have a Saviour who died so that those burdens can be lifted off of us. Anything we're still carrying is unnecessary weight. You were created by this amazing God, who designed you, just the way that you are, for a purpose. You're not an accident, you're not a mistake, you're made in the image of God. Get your eyes off yourself, and take a look at Him. Soon, those things won't matter so much.

A Bigger Picture

I wonder, over the course of our lifetime, how much time is taken up worrying; trying to impress other people, trying to live up to our own standards. It's said that girls do not dress to impress boys – girls dress to impress girls. I'm sure the same can be said about guys; guys do not spend hundreds on the latest pair of trainers to impress girls – they do it to live up to this image that they feel they need to fit in to. I wonder if we would like ourselves a lot more if we weren't so worried about these things; if we simply looked at the person that God had made us to be, and admired His creation for what it is.

Self-esteem is one of those funny words that no-one can really define specifically, but generally refers to the way that we feel about ourselves – confidence in one's own worth and abilities. I hold others in high esteem when they have qualities that I consider to be good – these could be physical qualities, or they could be things related to their character; and the same applies for myself. I have high self-esteem when I consider myself to have good qualities.

We know that image shouldn't be a major factor here, but it is. I feel a lot better about myself when I'm not having a bad-hair-day, when I've had time to throw on a bit of make-up and when I'm wearing clothes that I feel comfortable in. And, whether I'd like to admit it or not, image is a factor in the people that I choose to hold in high esteem. Generally, we pick people who look like us – in my case, white, middle class, slightly hipster girls in their twenties are the people that I hold up as having good qualities, and therefore want to spend a lot of my time with. This is a reflection on our culture as a whole, and can be so dangerous – if we only spend time with and esteem the people who look like us, sound like us and value the things that we say, we're not going to be challenged. While this is a comfortable place to sit in, it's not going to make us a better person.

When we see ourselves displaying good qualities, we feel better about ourselves – we have higher self-esteem. Whether these qualities are physical, or whether they're character traits like love, compassion, kindness and joy; the more I see them in myself, the better I feel about myself. Equally, if I see traits in myself that I consider to be bad qualities, I think less of myself and my self-esteem is likely to be lowered. My idea of what I am worth is lowered. So, the way that I feel about myself, and ultimately the way that I feel about other people, is based on a judgement; am I good, or am I bad?

The thing is, when it comes to the way that we look, if this is something that we struggle with, we often automatically jump to the *bad* judgement. That person on the front of the glossy magazine is better looking than me, and therefore I'm average, at best. My friend is so much prettier before she even puts on make-up, and yet I spend hours getting ready before I go out and still feel insecure. The way that we feel about how we look can affect the way that we feel about everything about ourselves – and ultimately, we end up letting our head talk us down, because we feel like we're not good enough.

When we find our value in the way that we look, we look around us to find the person who can make us relax by the way that they look. *At least I don't look like them.* When we find our value in the way that we look, we find that we must put on a character, and be super-outgoing, or super-funny, to make up for what we think is our deficit. When we find our value in the way that we look, we think that we cannot truly live until we look a certain way. When we find our value in the way that we look, we find that we are looking for the person who will love us "despite" the way that we look. When we find our value in the way that we look, we convince ourselves that a relationship just isn't necessary, and that we are OK on our own. When we find our value in the way that we look, we settle in being OK, because we feel that we will never be anything more than that.

That *average* door is so dangerous – because it keeps us in bondage, it keeps us in that place of not knowing our worth as children, created by God, made in His image.

God's Handiwork

For we are God's handiwork, created in Christ Jesus to do good works, which God prepared in advance for us to do. (Ephesians 2:10)

We are God's handiwork – He created us, on purpose, just as we are, for a reason. You are not a mistake. God didn't slip up when He created you. The Word says that you were created for a purpose – there's a reason that you're here and there's a job for you to do. Don't get me wrong; simply doing the right things doesn't make us valuable. We are valuable because we come from God, and because He loves us so much that He sent His Son to come and die for us. But our lives are so much bigger than just existing, and there's more important things than the way that we look. You're here on purpose!

Think of Mother Theresa, for example – a woman who dedicated her life to helping the sick, the widows and the orphans. She's famous, even by the worlds' standards: she's been invited to international events, TV interviews, and she's held up as one of the world's top female leaders. You wouldn't find her on the front of Vogue; but I bet there's not a single person in the world who would call Mother Theresa "average". She wasn't concerned with fitting in with the crowd, not standing out, making sure that no-one's got anything to say about her.

Instead, she took her eyes off herself, and looked at God, and the people that He had asked her to care for. Mother Theresa was beautiful because she was God's masterpiece, created new in Jesus to do His work. She has compassion for others. She was a servant, she was selfless, and she put the needs of others before her own. God used her unique gifts, the way that He made her, in a way that changed the world.

Samuel and Eliab

> *When they arrived, Samuel saw Eliab and thought, "Surely the Lord's anointed stands here before the Lord." But the Lord said to Samuel, "Do not consider his appearance or his height, for I have rejected him. The Lord does not look at the things that man looks at. People look at the outward appearance, but the Lord looks at the heart. (1 Samuel 16:6-7)*

While Eliab looked like the best option for King, God had anointed and called David for the job. Samuel immediately thought that Eliab was the person that God had chosen, and he didn't even consider anyone else.

But God set him straight, with a whisper into his soul: I don't look at the external appearance, I don't consider people in the same way that the world does. I look at the heart; I see wisdom, integrity, mercy and justice, and these are the things that please me. Throughout the Bible, we see God honouring and blessing those who have been least regarded by the world. David was the youngest of all his brothers, and he would not have been told that he was set to rule; he would have been seen as the least. His name means Beloved, and this is where his power came from: not from position or stature, but in being a beloved child of God.

But what about Jesus – do people think about His outward appearance, other than the fact that He was a man? No. Instead, he's memorialised in the image of Him hanging on a cross and dying. He's not remembered because of what He looked like, but because of what He did.

I wonder how often, in our culture, we ignore the David, and instead choose to invest in the Eliab? We think that the talent is in the one that looks the best, that performs the best on a surface level – but God says that He does not see these things; instead, He looks at the heart. We can choose whether we are going to look at people through human eyes, and pick the best based on external appearance or performance, or through God's eyes, and see the things of the heart that God truly sees. We cannot lean on our own understanding, but when we choose to look at people as God looks at them, we catch a glimpse of who they were created to be.

God does not favour young over old, blonde over brown, thin over big, old and wise over young and naïve. He favours those who have a heart for Him. When Jesus chose His twelve disciples, they were the lowest of the low; the unschooled, the fishermen. Jesus chose the people that nobody expected anything from, and invited them on an adventure with Him.

Let's lift our expectations of the ones that nobody is expecting anything from. We don't need to dress people up, or wait until they look a certain way before they are worth anything. For God does not look at the things that man looks at; God sees the heart, and He loves what He sees.

I Am Attractive

The lie that we're fighting against here is that feeling of ugliness when we look in the mirror, instantly noticing all the things that we don't like about ourselves. It's the feelings of inadequacy when we compare ourselves to other people, or to the image of beauty that we are bombarded with by the media.

So, know this, even if I'm the only voice that you're hearing say this right now: you are attractive. You are enough. The things that you notice about yourself that make you want to hide – they're not the things that other people notice about you. They're not the things that are important.

We read in the Bible that when God made the first people, Adam and Eve, He looked at the things that He had made and He said that it was *good*. Here, the word good comes from the word ***towb***; meaning beautiful. The phrase "it was good" can also be translated as "it was beautiful" – God is beauty, He creates beauty, and we are beautiful because we are created by this beautiful God. In God we find beauty that does not exist in the world; while it's tempting to look away, it's not worth it. Adam and Eve were tempted; tempted to eat fruit from the *tree of good and evil*. Here, we see the difference between God's beauty and the ugliness of things that are not from God; while it was tempting for Adam and Eve to eat the fruit from this tree, it showed them the ugliness that was in the world, and they were kept away from the beauty of God.

It's easy to look at others and envy the physical things they have; things that might seem appealing to the eye – but we have the beauty of God, which is far richer and better than all of the things that the world can offer. To envy the people that don't know God because they have good things is treating the things of this life bigger and better than God's love – putting more importance on physical good than moral. It makes us doubt that God rules the universe and that He loves us enough to provide for all our needs. Seeing their riches has the power to make us wonder if there is any point in religion, if we let it; and in fact, there isn't any point in religion – we have something far greater. Here's the truth:

Yet I am always with you; you hold me by my right hand. You guide me with your counsel, and afterwards you will take me into glory. Whom have I in heaven but you? And earth has nothing I desire but you. (Psalm 73:23-25)

So go, sit in front of a mirror, have a look at your face, have a poke and a prod and a stretch and a pull. Know that you were designed that way and that it is culture and the media that has told you that this isn't good enough. Know that God is looking at you with so much pride and joy in His eyes at all that He has created. Know that we are part of a bigger picture, a story that is so much bigger than the way that we look. We get to participate in God's great plan – and He made you, on purpose, exactly at the right time, for a moment such as this. Nothing Else Matters.

Questions for Reflection:

1. *On a scale of 1-10, how much would you say you currently struggle with insecurities in this area?*

2. *Would you walk through the "average" door, or the "attractive" door?*

3. *How does it feel to look in the mirror and have a look at your face?*

4. *Which Biblical truth are you going to choose to stand in in this area?*

CHAPTER FIVE
I AM STRONG

We live in a world of pretenders. So much of what we do comes from trying to live up to this person that we want the world to see us as. We create this person, this character, and the way that we speak and act and relate to other people comes from that person, rather than from who we really are. Maybe they're slightly cooler than we think we are, slightly more intelligent, more funny – maybe they're closer to God than we think we are.

And when we're living as this character, God is just a side-character in our plot. We make up our own lines, we have our own end-point that we want to get to, and we do it in the way that we want to: we don't really need God in that life at all. Christians sometimes talk about making Christ our saviour. But here's the thing: we cannot "accept" Jesus as our Saviour. Jesus is Saviour whether we accept Him or not. We accept Him as Lord, and accepting Him as Lord of our lives is what transforms us. We walk in newness of life; we are different to the person that we were before. All the fullness of God dwells in Christ; and therefore, dwells in us too, included in Him.

Strength from Faith

God is so faithful to us when we are making a journey for Him. He's not interested in being a side-character in the plot of our lives – He wants to be our main focus, for us to lean our whole selves on Him, and to find our strength in Him. I love these verses in the story of Moses leading the Israelites out of Egypt, as they're about to walk through the Red Sea:

They were totally afraid. They cried out in terror to God. They told Moses, "Weren't the cemeteries large enough in Egypt so that you had to take us out here in the wilderness to die? What have you done to us, taking us out of Egypt? Back in Egypt didn't we tell you this would happen? Didn't we tell you, 'Leave us alone here in Egypt — we're better off as slaves in Egypt than as corpses in the wilderness.'"

> *Moses spoke to the people: "Don't be afraid. Stand firm and watch God do his work of salvation for you today. Take a good look at the Egyptians today for you're never going to see them again.*
>
> *God will fight the battle for you. And you? You keep your mouths shut!"*
>
> *God said to Moses: "Why cry out to me? Speak to the Israelites. Order them to get moving. Hold your staff high and stretch your hand out over the sea: Split the sea! The Israelites will walk through the sea on dry ground." (Exodus 14:10-16, MSG)*

So, that's what Moses did. He walked straight up to the Red Sea, which was this huge obstacle in their path; he stretched out his hand, and God split the sea, so that the Israelites could walk through it, and escape the people who had kept them captive. I love the image of this group of slaves walking to freedom, right through an obstacle that seemed impossible to overcome. I bet the walk through that sea wasn't an easy one. I bet they were terrified – water towering high on either side of them. And it wasn't even an easy walk for them to physically take – they would have had to walk downhill, into the ocean bed; across, and then up again on the other side. Imagine the trust that it must have taken to walk downhill into an ocean bed, with everyone that you love, while water towers over you on both sides.

Sometimes we need to keep walking, taking the path that we would never take on our own, because we trust that God is going to protect us, no matter how impossible it looks. Sometimes, the only way for us to get through the circumstances that we are in is for God to come through for us. That's faith; trusting that God will show up, when there's no other way to make it through. Sometimes, like the Israelites, we have to take the path that looks the riskiest, the way that no-one else is going, because that's the right way. It's not an easy walk, and sometimes it involves walking down into the midst of trouble.

> ***"Don't be afraid. Stand firm and watch God do his work of salvation for you today. Take a good look at the Egyptians today, for you're never going to see them again. God will fight the battle for you."***
> *(Exodus 14:13, MSG)*

And here's what God did, after the Israelites had made it through the Red Sea: Moses stretched his hand out over the sea, and it went back into place, taking all of the Egyptians with it. God literally cleared the way for His people to come out of circumstances that were holding them in slavery, and then He slammed the door shut behind them, shutting the door on their past.

The Israelites came out the strongest in this situation, but they were not saved from the Egyptians by their own power – God was 100% in control. In our highest points and lowest points, we live by faith that God is who He says He is, and that He will do what He says He will do – that's strength.

This line from Paul begins to define what strength looks like in the life of a believer: ***"I can do all things, through Christ who strengthens me." (Philippians 4:13, NKJV[3])***

Now Paul was a cool guy. Before he became one of them, he hated Christians, locked them up, and beat them; then God turned him around and put him on a path talking to huge groups of people about how awesome God is. Paul is held up as one of the influential Christians ever; and he came from a place of hating the church. If you think that your past actions write you off from being used by God, let Paul assure you: you are definitely, absolutely, not that bad.

When Paul said this – "I can do all things, through Christ who strengthens me", he wasn't enjoying the highs of life. He was in prison – he had been locked up, beaten, tortured. So when he said that, he wasn't flying high, shouting about how he could do anything and how he was on top of the world – he was saying that even in his lowest moments, even when he was in prison and alone, he could get through it because of his faith in God.

This was faith that didn't stop when it was beaten down. It didn't stop when it seemed like there was no hope. It didn't stop when his circumstances didn't seem to match up with the things that God promises; I'd bet that while Paul was being beaten in prison, it didn't come easily to believe that God was protecting him, that He was going to continue to do great things through him. And yet it was easy to believe; Paul made the decision that his external circumstances were not going to beat him down – they weren't going to convince him that God is not all that He says He is.

I don't know if you know anyone like that – people who, even when they're going through the lowest point of their life, look to their faith for strength, and you can see God carrying them through. I look at these people and I see strength – but it's not their strength, it's God's strength, work-

---

[3] New King James Version

ing through them. And because they know that they can't get through it alone, they remember their identity, hidden in Him – and suddenly, they can do it, through the God who strengthens them.

My friend Ru is the epitome of strength, in my eyes. She's this kick-butt superstar from New Zealand: Mum of three beautiful girls, musician, teacher, supporter, friend, missionary; and her prayers would blow your socks off. I met Ru soon after moving to Cambridge, completely set-up by God: I was a lonely student who needed a family and a place to live, and Ru was the co-head of this incredible family, who had a heart for taking in the lonely and the wanderers and giving them a home. I lived with Ru, her family, and various lodgers for a year, and they absolutely became family.

Ru's girls are three of my favourite people on this planet; but, as you might expect, raising a family with three girls aged ten, seven and four comes with the odd moment of craziness. Ru recently told me the story of one particularly crazy afternoon: one girl was at a music lesson, one was at a birthday party, one wanted to be at home. All needed picking up at some point, Husband was working, house was being torn apart, dinner was not yet prepared; there was lots of work to be done and yet not enough time to do it. Definitely not time to sit down, alone, with God and just pray.

But Ru found herself in the car, on her own, just for a moment, while waiting for Daughter #1 to come out of her music lesson. "I just need you, God," she said out loud in the car. "I need your strength". She turned on the stereo – a worship CD that she'd heard a million times – rolled her seat back, closed her eyes, and just stopped for a second. "You've got five minutes, God," she thought. "Use these songs, find something in these words – I need you, Father".

Of course, He did it. What Father wouldn't grant a request like that? Daughter #1 hopped into the car, Ru sat up, got on with her day, and rocked it, with renewed strength from her heavenly Father. Those were five minutes that could have been spent sending the texts that she needed to, or calling her boss to organise things, or sorting out her calendar; but five minutes of just being willing to listen, and a desire to hear God, was all it took for her strength to be totally renewed in Him.

Good Days

Life is made up of all different kinds of days. Sometimes it feels like we're flying high, like nothing can touch us; sometimes it's more like we're just going through the motions, putting one foot in front of the other, doing what needs to be done. Some days, everything seems to be against us; we're fighting battles, one knock away from losing. And those battles don't just come one at a time – they don't just line up in front of us, until we're ready to take them on. They turn up unexpected on the good days, they overwhelm and disempower, and they can feel like they're crashing in on us from all sides. During the good days, it's easy to see that God is walking beside us; but at our worst, we can feel abandoned, out there on our own, walking through the fire and it can be hard to see where God is in that.

God speaks to us through Psalm 91:

"If you'll hold on to me for dear life," says God, "I'll get you out of any trouble. I'll give you the best of care, if you'll only get to know and trust me. Call me and I'll answer, be by your side in bad times; I'll rescue you, then throw you a party. I'll give you a long life, give you a long drink of salvation!" (Psalm 91:14-16, MSG)

God's making us a promise: that if we look to Him, if we cling on to Him, He'll protect us, rescue us, keep us out of trouble. When we call on God, He answers us; and suddenly the impossible is possible, and the situations that we thought would overcome us have been defeated. I love that God doesn't just rescue us – He throws us a party; He's ready to scoop us up into His arms.

I made a decision recently: to declare each day as a good day. I start the day with a decision that it **is** going to be a good day – that life is not going to overcome me; that it's not even going to be about just going through the motions but that I'm going to cling on to the promise that God has for me that if I call on Him, He'll answer me. When I look to God first, I look for the joy, the good, throughout the day. It's enough to get me through the overslept alarms, the bad hair days and the annoying moments. The day doesn't get a choice – it's going to be good, because I have a God who is good.

Psalm 145 says this:

I will exalt you, my God the King; I will praise your name forever and ever. Every day I will praise you, and extol your name forever and ever.

… They tell of the power of your awesome works – and I will proclaim your great deeds. They celebrate your abundant goodness, and joyfully sing of your righteousness. (Psalm 145:1, 6-7)

Just as God has made a promise to me, I'm making a promise to Him: that I will praise Him, tell of all the good things He has done for me. I'm not going to let a bad day decide how good my God is: instead, I'm going to let His goodness carry me through all kinds of days. And here's a declaration of praise that we are asked to make:

This is the day that the Lord has made; let us rejoice and be glad in it. (Psalm 118:24, ESV[4])

This psalm sings of the truth: this **is** the day that the Lord has made. The fact that God created this day means that He should be praised, and believing this is a simple matter of choice. The day has its being because of God, and therefore He is worthy to be praised: ***"You are worthy, our Lord and God, to receive glory and honour and power, for you created all things, and by you they were created and have their being." (Revelation 4:11).*** The other half of the verse is a decision to act on our part: let us rejoice and be glad in it – simply because of the truth that God has created it.

The psalm doesn't say ***let us rejoice, if everything works out alright.*** It doesn't say ***this is the day that the Lord has made, but I can't rejoice because my circumstances are too difficult.*** It doesn't say ***I might rejoice for a while later when I'm feeling better.*** It says ***let us rejoice and be glad;*** God is good and He is worthy of praise, whether our circumstances reflect that or not.

Truth is truth is truth, and while our experience of reality is based on our changing perceptions of our circumstances, His truth does not change. The truth is, we are holy and blameless, marked with a seal, hidden in Him and new creations because Christ died for us. While our reality may be that we feel ourselves messing up, we feel guilty, we feel dirty, we don't feel strong enough, the truth is that our strength comes from God, who has redeemed us. The old creation has no right to be here anymore, for we are new creations in Christ: the old has gone and the new is here!

Participating in His Nature

To those who through the righteousness of our God and Saviour Jesus Christ have received a faith as precious as ours: Grace and peace be yours in abundance through the knowledge of God and of Jesus our Lord. (2 Peter 1:1-2)

---

[4] English Standard Version

This part of the Bible would have originally been written in Greek, and over time, it's been translated into every language – English being one of them. This is incredible, because it means that we have access to everything that was written; but, like Chinese Whispers, it might mean that we can't see the picture as clearly as it was first written. When you think about knowledge, you might think about what you can learn from books, but that's not what Paul was talking about here: he's talking about an **experience** of Jesus. So, through an experience and a knowledge of Jesus that is deeper than simply what we have in our heads, **grace and peace are ours in abundance**. With an encounter with Jesus comes abundant grace and peace; grace and peace that is not dependant on our circumstance, but on our knowledge of Jesus Christ. This is not even knowledge that comes from reading the Bible and sitting in great church services; it's knowledge that comes from a real, first-hand relationship. This knowledge transforms us.

His divine power has given us everything we need for a godly life through our knowledge of him who called us by his own glory and goodness. Through these he has given us his very great and precious promises, so that through them you may participate in the divine nature, having escaped the corruption in the world caused by evil desires. (2 Peter 1:3-4)

Here's the thing about something that has already been given to me: **I can't mess it up.** Sometimes we live in a pattern of begging God for things: for faith, for patience, for health, for the finances we need. But here, we read that His divine power **has given** us everything that we need for a godly life – through this experiential knowledge that comes through a first-hand relationship with Him. He's not waiting for us to ask before He gives us these things – He's already given them to us. We have them. He has given us everything we need for a godly life, and He has given us His very great and precious promises.

Everything that God promises us in the Bible **has already been given to us.** We're going to go on to look at some of these promises a little bit later, but this I've learnt: **I do not need to wait for God to give me something, because He already has**. I don't need to pray that God will be with me, because He promises that He is with me – which means He already is.

And I'm not stagnant in this – He has given me His great and precious promises, **so that I might participate in the divine nature**. I have a part and a role to play in God's kingdom, and in His plans on the earth, not because of who I am, but because of what He's given me. God wants you to be a part of things – we're called to participate in all that He's doing, and to make this possible, He's **given us everything that we need.**

For this very reason, make every effort to add to your faith goodness; and to goodness, knowledge; and to knowledge, self-control; and to self-control, perseverance; and to perseverance, godliness; and to godliness, mutual affection; and to mutual affection, love. For if you possess these qualities in increasing measure, they will keep you from being ineffective and unproductive in your knowledge of our Lord Jesus Christ. But whoever does not have them is near-sighted and blind, forgetting that they have been cleansed from their past sins. (2 Peter 1:5-9)

This is not about having to live up to these things, or risk God not loving me any more, but these things are the fruit of living in the knowledge of Jesus Christ. Think about a seed: if I plant an apple pip, a tree will grow, and fruit grows. This knowledge is the seed in us, that promises to produce fruit in us. These characteristics are all great things; but we can't fake them. They come from this relationship with Christ, from our characters being in line with His spirit. I don't know about you, but I don't have the capacity to have all of these things, all the time, in my own strength: I need Jesus. Because when I'm in Him, it isn't my character that shines through: I am hidden in Him; I'm dead, and He lives in me.

When we accept our salvation, our old man dies, and we become a new creation, hidden in Him: *"Therefore, if anyone is in Christ, the new creation has come. The old has gone, the new is here!" (2 Corinthians 5:17)* All of my characteristics died with me: bitterness, selfishness, anger, mistrust. I'm hidden in Christ, and His character has become my own – all of these are mine to claim: knowledge, self-control, perseverance, godliness, mutual affection, love. If I know my identity and walk hidden in Christ, it's His character that's on display. The enemy has no power to call out my old character, because it's covered by Him. But as soon as I talk about my old self, and put that on display, the enemy has a foothold to come in and point it out. It's my choice.

Like Paul says: if anyone does not have these qualities, they are short sighted and blind, and forgetting that they has been forgiven from past sins. It's so easy to find our identity in our past selves, to get clouded vision and to forget this great knowledge we have of Jesus Christ – making us short-sighted and blind.

Imagine living every moment of your day fully in the knowledge of what Jesus has done for you, and walking fully in all of these things. Knowledge. Self-control. Perseverance. Godliness. Mutual affection. Love.

The devil is not smart. He looks for the obvious things – the things that we put on display that he can trip us up on. But, as long as we talk about Jesus, and our identity in Him as a new creation, the devil can't find us –

we're hidden in Him. The old creation is only here as long as we keep talking about it; so keep your eyes on that new creation, kid – you've got this.

Strength in Inarticulation

The words of a friend are carved forever in my mind, bringing those warm fuzzy feelings to the surface every time I think of them. We were sat in a coffee shop during quite a difficult time in my life, a time when everything was thrown at me at the same time; it felt like for a few weeks, life became more about surviving than thriving, just about putting one foot in front of the other and making it through another day. We had talked, and prayed, and cried, and talked some more, and then she said to me "you know, in all of this Heaths; I know you are feeling weak right now, but all I can see is your strength". Those words, amid a time when people looked at me with pitying eyes and tutted while helping me up off the ground, told me that someone got it. She understood – she knew that this wasn't who I was. She knew my identity was not found in my weakness but in the strength that showed up in putting one foot in front of the other and carrying on. She's the friend that I do not have to have my act together to be able to talk to – I can turn up and say what I want to say, and not say what I do not want to say, and know that she is totally on my team.

But there are parts of me, parts of all of us, that nobody gets to see. There are times that nobody gets to help us through because they are not open for public viewing. For most the time, we only call on a friend for help when we can articulate what we want to see, and when we can see the possibility of coming out on top at the other end. We edit the things that we want to say; we shape it in a way that they will understand and be able to give us a solution to. And then our spirit becomes clouded with all the things that we have not said, and everything that is left to be expressed.

There is strength in relationships in which we can say everything that we need to say, without saying words. These friendships are a rarity; but we find this in a relationship with our Father.

The Spirit helps us in our weakness. We do not know what we ought to pray for, but the Spirit himself intercedes for us through wordless groans. (Romans 8:26)

God loves it when we turn to Him, and in the times when we do not know what to say, He fills in the gaps. He does not see our weakness as a barrier or an issue, but He swoops us up from this place, and articulates the things that we cannot articulate. There are shallow feelings that can be expressed through words, but language breaks down in the expression of deep pain, our deepest emotions or our truest love. But consider how deep is a relationship when there is complete understanding without words; when two connect at a heart level and these things are just taken from one to the other.

In the matters of our deepest emotions, our deepest hurt and expressing our love for God, we don't usually know what is going on enough to be able to express it: we see things on a surface level, and so deal with surface-level problems. But we have a God who knows our heart more that we could possibly know; who, when we let Him, takes these burdens from us and replaces our weakness with His strength.

Abraham

A little bit later in the story of Abraham, we read this story of faith and trust, when Abraham is called by God to go to a place he doesn't know:

> ***By faith Abraham, when called to go to a place he would later receive as his inheritance, obeyed and went, even though he did not know where he was going. By faith he made his home in the promised land like a stranger in a foreign country; he lived in tents, as did Isaac and Jacob, who were heirs with him of the same promise. For he was looking forward to the city with foundations, whose architect and builder is God.***
> ***(Hebrews 11:8-10)***

Abraham went on a journey with God, simply because God told him to go, even though he didn't fully know where he was going, or where he would end up. That's faith – to set off, heading for a land where you know you're not welcome or wanted, without any idea of why you're going; to live in tents as an alien in that country, relying the whole time on the goodness of God.

He eventually made it all the way to Canaan, the promised land, and I love these words: "for he was looking forward to the city with foundations, whose architect and builder is God". It wasn't an easy journey on the way to the promised land, and Canaan wasn't an easy place to be once he was there – but Abraham made it, because he had his eyes fixed on a bigger picture. Canaan wasn't the final destination, it wasn't the end goal: Abraham knew that there was a much bigger goal in God, which made all of the earthly challenges he faced seem tiny.

Faith does not stop. Abraham could have stopped at any point along the journey, but he pressed through; not because of Canaan, but because of God. Canaan wasn't the important place to him: he was heading for a city whose architect and builder was God, and that was a far greater goal. He had faith that God was going to bless him, and that his journey was heading somewhere, but he also knew who God was – and sometimes, that's enough.

Strength here means looking at the end goal – the city greater than anything on earth, whose architect and builder is God – and letting that sight guide us through the things that we have to walk through. Faith means not giving up when everything seems to be stacked against us, because the truth is bigger than what our circumstances are telling us. Strength is not relying on the answers that we can see in ourselves, but knowing that we need to exercise faith to see things happen.

Life can sometimes feel like we're walking through without any idea where we are going; but this is all part of the adventure. Abraham had his eyes set over the skyline, on a city that was bigger and better than anywhere that he was heading on earth, and that meant that he could enjoy the journey without worrying about whether it made sense or not, because he knew that God was at the other end. He found his strength not in having every step planned out for himself, but in knowing that God was walking every step with him. Anything that we could possibly achieve here on earth is not the final goal, but part of the adventure that we are on with God, who we get to spend an eternity with.

Questions for Reflection:

1. *What circumstances or trials have caused you to wobble in your walk with God?*

2. *What trials would currently have the potential to cause you to wobble?*

3. *What truth are you going to stand on in those trials?*

CHAPTER SIX
I AM CAPABLE

The accusation of incompetence is one of the biggest lies that we need to fight against to be effective in the Kingdom of God. There is an enemy, and although he only has the power that we give him in our lives, he is sneaky: he hits us where it hurts most, in ways that will make us feel unable to move. For a lot of us, feeling incompetent freezes us: we remember the times that we have messed up, and this holds us in bondage and puts us in fear of trying again. We don't move, we don't put ourselves in situations where we might fail, because we're afraid of what might happen.

But here's the truth that we need to speak over our circumstances when we come up against feelings of incompetence: our competence does not come from ourselves, but from God. I am competent because I am created, and I am a child of God. When I do things, it is not in my own strength but God's: I am adequate because God is adequate. We are hidden in Him, so our strength is His strength; our competence is His competence:

Not that we are competent in ourselves to claim anything for ourselves, but our competence comes from God. (2 Corinthians 3:5)

When we worry about whether we are good enough to do something, we are trying to take the control away from God and do it in our own strength. Because the truth is that we are not good enough – we are not adequate apart from the power of God. Sometimes, we confuse humility with worrying. Humility does not say "I'm not good enough for this," it says: "I need God for this".

This is the truth of who we are, that we can put over our perception of the circumstances that we are in: we are not inadequate and we are not incompetent, but we are more than adequate because our adequacy comes from God, who has given it to us freely. Therefore, when things come up against us and we feel inadequate, we have the word of truth to speak over the circumstances, and to help us remember our identity hidden in Christ.

Do your best to present yourself to God as one approved, a worker who does not need to be ashamed and who correctly handles the word of truth.

(2 Timothy 2:15)

And therefore I do not need to be ashamed, or feel like I am not good enough, because I know that I am good enough. The word of truth is my weapon in this – whatever everything else around me looks like, I can use the Word as a sword, and know that I am approved by God. This isn't easy, and it takes diligence; I need to make the decision to use this over and over again, every time I come up against something that tries to shout over the truth.

Joshua

We have a God who does not leave us alone when we are walking into a difficult situation; but that does not mean that we won't need to take ground. I love the story of Joshua. As we read at the beginning of the book of Joshua, Moses had died, having led the Israelites out of captivity in Egypt, and Joshua was the leader that God had chosen to lead the people into the promised land that God had prepared for them.

At the beginning of Joshua 1, God is giving a little pep-talk to the man that he had chosen to lead:

"Moses my servant is dead. Now then, you and all these people, get ready to cross the Jordan river into the land that I am about to give to them – to the Israelites. I will give you every place where you set your foot,"… "No-one will be able to stand against you all the days of your life." … "Then you will be prosperous and successful. Have I not commanded you? Be strong and courageous" (Joshua 1:2-9)

God had big plans for Joshua and his men, but He was accompanying them with big promises; God was making them strong and mighty, and it was therefore His strength that their enemies were up against. God keeps His promises, and this guaranteed Joshua and his men their safety through a journey that must have seemed pretty scary from the beginning. Also, God didn't just make sure that they scraped through, He promised that they would prosper, and that they would have everything that they need, because He was looking after them.

Courage that does not rely on Christ is foolish, and will fall at some point, as impossible circumstances come our way. But when we lean on God and find our strength and courage in His strength, it is Him that gets us through. He promises that He can do more than we can ask or imagine.

He says that with Him, all things are possible: this is the God on who we can rely for our strength.

He promised Joshua that He would give him every place that he placed his foot, and this promise extends to us. God is there, He is with us and He is doing the work for us, but we need to move – we need to put our foot somewhere. Life becomes about trying things out, going in different directions, putting our feet on new ground for God, and watching to see what He can do in and through us. He promises us that we will be prosperous and successful; this is not necessarily in material gain – that idea of prospering only stands up in our middle class, Western world. He will make us prosper in the things that really matter: in peace, joy, comfort, contentment, and our success will be in the things that we see Him do through us in the places that we set our feet.

"God often opens his hand by one finger at a time, and leaves us face to face with some plain but difficult duty, without letting us see the helps to its performance, 'til we need to use them" (MacLaren[5]) Sometimes the path is only revealed part at a time; and of course, God is there to help us, but we need to see part of the path to realise that we need God's help. In this case, Joshua knew that they needed God's help to overcome the things that they were facing, but that they had this promise of wonderful things tomorrow.

Sometimes we just need the courage to step out of our comfort zone. We tend to associate courage with extreme action – slaying the dragon, defeating the enemy, fighting the battle – but courage is day-to-day. It's keeping going, it's telling the truth, it's asking for help when we know that we need it, and it's making a change, one step at a time. Joshua and his men were walking through the desert. This place was becoming familiar to them, and I bet it was tempting for them to stay in that place, but they had been called on, for *tomorrow* God was going to do great things: ***"Consecrate yourselves for tomorrow the Lord will do amazing things among you." (Joshua 3:5)*** The stretching of our trust happens when we're on the journey – when we're in the comfort zone, and we have the choice of whether to keep going, or to stop where we are. And when we are faithful on the journey, it's amazing to see the doors that God opens for the next stretch.

---

[5] MacLaren, A., *'Expositions of Holy Scripture'*, The Book of Joshua, Chapter 3

God's strength and power are shown in our weakness – when we reach the end of our ability, He steps in, shows up and shows off. We see this all the way through the story of Joshua, who knew that the task that he had been given, to lead the Israelites into the promised land, was not one that he had to do on his own, but something that God had given him to do. This is the promise that God gave Joshua at the beginning of the story:

> **Be strong and courageous, because you will lead these people to inherit the land that I swore to their forefathers to give them. (Joshua 1:6)**

God had promised His people the land – their only job was to step into it.

> **Do nothing out of selfish ambition or vain conceit. Rather, in humility value others above yourselves. (Philippians 2:3)**

The second that we accept the love of God and say yes to His calling and adventure, we lose the right to make life about ourselves. God has made each one of us capable and useful for His will – this isn't about us anymore, but the fruit that we are producing. He has made us capable to *go*; and usually, we are the only thing that is getting in our way. Or, we try and keep control of the things we are doing, and attempt to make God's plans fit into our neat lives.

I really like lists. I make a to-do list every day, of the tasks I would like to accomplish. I write shopping lists and stick to them to the letter. I have lists on my phone, on my fridge, next to my bed. Ticking off that first task of the day is one of the best feelings. When it comes down to it, I make lists because I like to know what I'm doing, when I'm doing it and what's next. I like to know that I'm in control of my day – that everything is ticking along nicely.

And that, I think, is why God turns everything on its head every now and then. My neat lists get put to one side, and I must trust in Him that He will use my day for His will. When that happens, I get the privilege of helping people through tough times, of praying with people in need, of seeing people inspired and full of joy, of sitting down and getting to hear awesome stories, and of achieving things that definitely weren't on my nice neat lists. I see sessions that I had planned turned around, and things happen that I couldn't have thought of. My plans don't even compare.

Someone once said that *"the best self-preservation is to commit ourselves to God's keeping." (Henry[6])* As much as I try, I can't save myself – I can't guarantee that nothing bad is ever going to happen. But when I choose to trust in God, I don't need to go anywhere else, or rely on anyone else for protection – nothing else compares. I can do this with entire confidence that God has got my back, and I can expect God to turn up. However much I try to have my own life sorted and planned, it could all fall apart in a moment. But leaning my life on God gives me the strength to make it through things that I wouldn't have a chance of getting through on my own.

David, the writer of the Psalms, once wrote a prayer to God:

Guard my life, for I am faithful to you; save your servant who trusts in you. You are my God; have mercy on me, Lord, for I call to you all day long. Bring joy to your servant, Lord, for I put my trust in you. (Psalm 86:2-4)

God absolutely does not have to help us, but He does. Why? He helps us because we are holy in His sight. That part of the psalm has also been translated as *"preserve my life, for I am holy – I am sanctified by grace and devoted to your service"*. When David called himself holy, he was not saying he was perfect. We can't be perfect; we mess up, we make mistakes and we do not match up to God's standards.

But holiness = grace + devotion to God. David was looking to God for protection because he was a friend of God, and he knew that he was covered by God's grace. He didn't have a right to a relationship with God because he was **good** – he knew that he wasn't good enough and that he needed grace. He had devoted himself to God, and so he looked to God for protection when he was in danger. A child will look to a parent for protection, because they are a child; we look at the law for protection because we are citizens; and the people of God can look to Him for protection because we are His people.

I do not come to God on my own merit. I come to Him in the knowledge that my own merit is not enough, but that His grace covers me and He sees me as holy. He is my Father and I'm His daughter – I'm walking with Him not because of what I've done, but because of who He is. When we accept the salvation that He gives us, we are made holy and

---

[6] Henry, M., *'Matthew Henry's Concise Commentary on the Bible'*, Psalm 86

blameless in His sight: not because we have made ourselves that way, but because of who He is.

God helps us, because **He is holy**. Psalm 18:30 says this: ***"God's way is perfect. All the LORD's promises prove true. He is a shield for all who look to him for protection."***. We have a big, big God, and He is perfect; He can't be bad, He can't sin. And God takes this perfection, and through Jesus, paints it over us, so that His perfection covers our imperfection. We can't earn God's love – there's nothing that we can do to get us to God's level. But His flawlessness covers our flaws.

And God helps us because **we are loved.** We have a promise from God – that He *will* hear us when we call – and He will listen. He is compassionate – He sees our hearts, He sees when we are hurting and burdened, and He hears us call. He's seen it all – there's nothing that we can do that will make Him love us any less.

He doesn't need us to try to be perfect – He wants us to see that we're not, and to look to Him to help. There's no point in trying to do it by ourselves – we can't save ourselves. But when we look to Him, He will be our shield and our protector, and will give us the strength to carry on.

<u>Jars of Clay</u>

But we have this treasure in jars of clay to show that this all-surpassing power is from God and not from us. We are hard pressed on every side, but not crushed; perplexed, but not in despair; persecuted, but not abandoned; struck down, but not destroyed. We always carry around in our body the death of Jesus, so that the life of Jesus may also be revealed in our body. (2 Corinthians 4:7-10)

Corinth, in the time that this letter was written, was one of the biggest manufacturers of clay jars: containers hand-made by skilled potters, shaped and molded, and then baked until it was hard. Sometimes, the jars were decorated, painted or glazed, and would have been sold. Valuable things were kept in these jars: they could hold liquids, or hide things like scrolls or valuable documents. But clay jars are breakable. They were temporary holding places – nothing could be kept in them forever.

Paul says that we are like jars of clay; in the natural, we are weak and feeble, we break and bend, and we don't last forever. Our bodies are beautiful, functional and breakable, but we have been designed and created, molded together by God, with a different purpose in mind for each of us.

But He has put treasure inside us; and this treasure is not temporary, but it will last forever. The treasure that we hold is the knowledge of God, and of His glory that is displayed through Christ; and, as these verses describe, we hold this treasure to show that in everything we do, the power comes from Him and not from us. We are just vessels that hold God's great glory and purpose; that is what makes us capable. We hold it to show that God is at work in us; our lives should not make sense apart from God.

The letter goes on to rip apart some of the lies that we are force-fed by the enemy: we are not crushed, not despairing, not abandoned, not destroyed. There are things that may come at us that are not from God but from the world – we may be hard-pressed, perplexed, persecuted, struck down – but we will not be overcome because we carry the death and life of Jesus in our bodies, that He might live through us.

There is humility in knowing that because our competence does not come from ourselves but from God, our purpose is to show the glory of God through our lives. The pressure is taken from us to be super-holy, super-amazing and productive for God, because it is not about our talent and ability anyway. Therefore, when we are hard-pressed on every side by the pressures of life, it is not our own power that saves us, but God's. The world can press on us, but it is not strong enough to overcome God's strength. The world can try to perplex us, but we have the truth of God that brings clarity and insight. The world can persecute us, but we have an ever-present Father who promises that He will never abandon us. It can strike us down, but we have the power of God in us, who sustains us.

Although we break and bend and do not last forever, we are vessels that hold this incredible glory and power of God. The things inside us are not of ourselves, but of the all-strong, all-powerful, awesome God that we have.

Remember This

Remember this: Whoever sows sparingly will also reap sparingly, and whoever sows generously will also reap generously. Each of you should give what you have decided in your heart to give, not reluctantly or under compulsion, for God loves a cheerful giver. And God is able to bless you abundantly, so that in all things at all times, having all that you need, you will abound in every good work. (2 Corinthians 9:6-8)

We often talk about these verses in the context of giving money, and receiving blessing, but this is not all that Paul was talking about here; of all the resources that we have, there are three that it is possible for us to give: treasure (money and possessions), time, and talents.

We make a decision in our heart, about the extent to which we give to God. If we decide that we are giving our all to God, that we are all-out living for him, it is going to affect the way that we use those three things. We'll give our time to serving God and loving other people. We'll give our talents and gifts in a way that bring glory to God and help us to be effective in the Kingdom. And we'll invest our money in places that God can use, and that help and bless people. We decide to what extent we are going to give these things: we can decide to go all-out for God, or to try and keep all of these things for ourselves. But: whoever sows sparingly will reap sparingly, and whoever sows generously will reap generously.

And here's the promise: that God will **make all grace abound to you**. God loves it when we trust in Him, and our lives echo this trust, and He comes to meet us in that. God is a generous God, and a life with Him is a fulfilled one:

> *For no matter how many promises God has made, they are "Yes" in Christ. And so through him the "Amen" is spoken to us by the glory of God. Now it is God who makes both us and you stand firm in Christ. He anointed us, set his seal of ownership on us, and put his Spirit in our hearts as a deposit, guaranteeing what is to come. (2 Corinthians 1:20-22)*

All grace will abound to me through Christ. Life is not about following some idea of God, and trying to be a good person along the way. He's a person, and I have His spirit in me – I am not an orphan, I am not unlovable, and I am not alone. I am a daughter of God and He is my Daddy. I don't have to strive to do the right thing every day – He's put His seal of ownership on me and I get love, joy, peace, kindness, grace abounding, just by being in Him. All of the promises He has made are Yes and Amen in Him!

This goes back to the image of God that we have in our head. If God was a far-off, strict, Morgan-Freeman-type character, then we would not have the same kind of relationship with Him; but our God is a good, good Father who has already said "Yes and Amen" to every desire that you have on your heart. He knows what you desire, and He wants to give you good gifts – and He promises that He will give you every place that you will set your foot. How much fun is this life with God?!

"So that in **all** things at **all** times, having **all** that you need, you will abound in every good work"; we won't just scrape through in the things that we try. I am not a failure; I will abound in every good work, because I have all that I need in all things at all times. God wants me to succeed in the things that I am doing for Him, and He has made me capable to do that. So therefore *"such confidence we have through Christ before God. Not that we* *are competent in ourselves to claim anything for ourselves, but our competence comes from God." (2 Corinthians 3:4-5)* I have life because God gives me life: everything that I have comes from God, and He is the Lord of my life, not me. I am competent because He is competent; I achieve because He goes before me. May our lives reflect the glory back at God, telling the world of all the things that He has done for, and in us.

Know When to Stop

I went to visit my parents last Christmas, and I went out on my own, on a walk through a local forest that I spent a lot of time in as a child. There had been a lot that I felt that I needed to process from the last year, and I often think best when I'm out on my own on a walk; so I hopped in my car and drove around the corner to the forest, in my wellies and an old hoodie. I asked God to speak to me about the things that He'd put on my heart, and just began walking, deciding to see what happened. The first thought that popped into my head was how different that day was from the day that I had walked that path before. The path was familiar, but I wasn't running along it as a child or a moody teenager: I was tracing my own footsteps as a semi-functional, mature adult.

The path was muddy the whole way, but I got to a point where the path was completely swamped, with only a tiny amount of dry ground around the edge of it. I could have risked trying to get across it and keep going, but as I stopped for a moment, I decided that it wasn't necessary, and turned back, still chatting away to God.

It struck me how much of a growth this was; I didn't try to carry on, just to be able to say that I'd walked a long way – that wasn't the important thing. Instead, I turned back, still doing the thing that I had set out to do. It struck me how, sometimes, it's tempting to try and go the "extra mile"; not in a good sense, but with the things that we are doing for God, with the intention that people can see how much we've done. We get praised when it seems like we're doing a lot for God; we're recognised as good. But this isn't necessarily for the right reasons – it's to try and gain people's approval and affection.

Let me tell you that it is totally acceptable to not be a "cover-girl/cover-boy" Christian – the people that we can often tend to compare ourselves to. God is not impressed by how good I look; He's concerned about whether the things that we do are for Him. Sometimes, the people who look the best put the most effort into it, striving and trying to look good; and frankly, it's not worth the effort. Integrity here is to follow God with all of our heart, and to not concern ourselves with the things that people say about us.

I turned back on my walk, and after a while hit a side path, which I didn't recognise, but looked a lot dryer than the main path ahead, which was getting muddy again. Not entirely sure why I was doing it, I found myself turning off onto the road less beaten – obviously off the main path.

Catching myself again, I realised how this is often what walking with God looks like; while taking the road less beaten, for me, used to be all about independence, it was now all about dependence on my Father, rather than following the crowd. As we're walking through life, it would often be easier for us to stay on the main path; but, when we follow His calling out, we will know that we're on the right path. It won't always be easy; we won't always feel instantly accepted, and it's scary sometimes, but ultimately, we're always better off in His will.

__Enter through the narrow gate. For wide is the gate and broad is the road that leads to destruction, and many enter through it. But small is the gate and narrow the road that leads to life, and only a few find it.__   *__(Matthew 7:13-14)__*

Co-Mission

This is exactly what God is calling us into; a mission that is not just ours, based on our own plans, but a mission that is joint with Him. A mission that doesn't necessarily look like the "easiest" option; but boy, is it worth it.

Before Jesus went to the cross to die, He called His disciples together to talk about the mission that He was leaving them with. The people followed Him up on to the mountain, some of them doubting and wondering what was about to happen; but when He turned and approached them, and spoke to them as a familiar voice, all those fears and doubts faded away, and they worshipped Him.

__Then the eleven disciples went to Galilee, to the mountain where Jesus had told them to go. When they saw him, they worshiped him; but some doubted. Then Jesus came to them and said, "All authority in heaven and on earth has been given to me. Therefore go and make disciples of all nations, baptising them in the name of the Father and of the Son and of the Holy__

Spirit, and teaching them to obey everything I have commanded you. And surely I am with you always, to the very end of the age.(Matthew 28:16-20)

He gave them a commission – literally, a co-mission with Him: we are not doing this by ourselves, but with the power and authority of Jesus. The power that is in me is the power that raised Jesus from the dead – when He was raised, I was raised. It was this power that raised Jesus from the dead, from the deepest parts of hell; it was this power that resurrected His body and then ascended Him in to heaven; this is some mighty power, and it now lives in me.

When we read the Word, and hear the things that God says about us, and the things that He is calling us to do, we are required to make an active choice; am I going to stay the way I was, or am I going to let this change me? We need to keep moving forwards with God, putting one foot in front of the other in faith; for we are not just hearers of the word, but doers of the word.

This power that we have is far above the powers and principalities; the things that try to overcome us. Jesus said that **all** authority on heaven and on earth has been given to Him; and if He has all the power, then they have none. Similarly, if He has all of the power, then without Him, we have none; but we are not without Him any more, but hidden in Him. All authority in heaven and on earth has been given to Him – and He is in us!

For this reason I remind you to fan into flame the gift of God, which is in you through the laying on of my hands. For the Spirit God gave us does not make us timid, but gives us power, love and self-discipline.   *(2 Timothy 1:6-7)*

So, if we are on a co-mission with God, and if our competence does not come from ourselves but from Him, then there are things that God has put inside us that help us to participate in this great plan that God has for us. Our culture tells us that thinking about the good things in ourselves – the things that we are great at and that can contribute to the world around us – is somehow bragging or arrogant. It's a culture that tells us not to boast, not to stand out, unless we are considered worthy of the attention by other people – and then we elevate these people so high that no-one can live up to their standards. We put people on pedestals, and allow ourselves to be kept in the boxes that society has put us in.

We are all totally unique; no one person is like the next and we all bring something totally different to contribute to the world. We bring different experiences, a different perspective; we bring different passions and a different way of expressing the things that we are passionate about. We bring different talents, different skills and interests. Together, we form a great, bigger picture:

Each of you should use whatever gift you have received to serve others, as faithful stewards of God's grace in its various forms. If anyone speaks, they should do so as one who speaks the very words of God. If anyone serves, they should do so with the strength God provides, so that in all things God may be praised through Jesus Christ. To him be the glory and the power forever and ever. Amen. (1 Peter 4:10-11)

When we use the gifts and the creativity that God has given us to serve others, we get to give them **God's grace**. God is glorified through the things that we do and the things that we create. It's a waste if we do not use these gifts and talents to serve others; God has given them to us, and He expects them to use them. Whenever we do, it's worship to Him as our Creator; and He is pleased with us.

We do it in His strength, because He is the one that created us, and gave us the ability to create. When we speak, we have the power to speak words of life and joy and light into people's lives; when we serve, we can look to God as the source of our strength to keep us going. When we do these things for God, we are bringing God glory, that He may be praised. Life with God is not boring, it's about living outrageously and loving outrageously; not for our glory, but His.

Jeremiah

In the book of Jeremiah, we read the story of Jeremiah the prophet, who had a specific calling on his life from God, and did some awesome things for God and His Kingdom. We read some of the conversations that God and Jeremiah had, working out his calling:

The word of the Lord came to me, saying, "Before I formed you in the womb I knew you, before you were born I set you apart; I appointed you as a prophet to the nations." "Alas, Sovereign Lord," I said, "I do not know how to speak; I am too young." (Jeremiah 1:4-6)

Jeremiah was a prophet – he was given a gift from God, to go and speak His word to the people. But ultimately, Jeremiah was a normal human being, and when he was given this task, he didn't feel up to it: "I am too young" – I haven't been equipped in how to speak, I don't have the skills to do this task that you have given me.

But God knew Jeremiah before he was even thought of: He formed him in the womb, and He knew everything about Jeremiah before he was even born. Had God made a mistake, by telling him he was appointed to be a prophet to the nations? Had He got that wrong, had He asked the wrong person? No! God had picked him out – it didn't have anything to do with who Jeremiah was, but who God was. God does not call the qualified, but He qualifies the called. He doesn't wait until we've learned all the skills by ourselves, nor does He only pick out those that could do the job in their own strength; but He knew each of us before we were born, and He has a plan and a purpose for our lives.

But the Lord said to me, "Do not say, 'I am too young.' You must go to everyone I send you to and say whatever I command you. Do not be afraid of them, for I am with you and will rescue you," declares the Lord. Then the Lord reached out his hand and touched my mouth and said to me, "I have put my words in your mouth. See, today I appoint you over nations and kingdoms to uproot and tear down, to destroy and overthrow, to build and to plant." (Jeremiah 1:7-10)

So this is the challenge we have from God: don't question His judgement, don't doubt that He has got the right person – He has known us since before we were born. Instead, know that God is working through us, He is with us, and He is not relying on our own skills and abilities to get the job done, but on our trust in Him. We don't need to fear the things that we are going out to do, because He's with us, and He rescues us.

God reached down and touched Jeremiah's mouth – the God who breathed the stars into existence and put them in the sky bent down to comfort and encourage Jeremiah, in the way that a parent would encourage their child. God does not set us up for failure; He puts the words in our mouth that we need, He gives us the skills that we need to get the job done, and He is with us.

As we've discussed, our human nature, our brain, has a habit of trying to shout over our heart when it comes to the things that God is asking us to do, or the dreams and ideas that we have from God. Our head, wounded by past experiences and times when we have failed, cuts through the leaping of our heart; we're taken back to all of the things that we can't do, all of the reasons that these things couldn't be possible.

But we have a creative God, who put us here on earth to actively participate in His creation – we were born on purpose, with a purpose, for a purpose, to make a difference; and in God, we are capable of amazing things. God knew exactly what He was doing when He created you. He knew where you were going to live, He knew who you were going to hang out with, and He knew the dreams and aspirations that you would have, because He planted them in your mind.

What, then, shall we say in response to these things? If God is for us, who can be against us? He who did not spare his own Son, but gave him up for us all — how will he not also, along with him, graciously give us all things? Who will bring any charge against those whom God has chosen? It is God who justifies. Who then is the one who condemns? No one. Christ Jesus who died — more than that, who was raised to life — is at the right hand of God and is also interceding for us. Who shall separate us from the love of Christ? Shall trouble or hardship or persecution or famine or nakedness or danger or sword?...

No, in all these things we are more than conquerors through him who loved us. (Romans 8:31-37)

We have a God who has so much crazy, ridiculous love for us that He sent His son to die so that He could have a relationship with us. This God has got our backs! He didn't do that out of duty – He did it because He loves us; how can this God not give us the desires of our hearts? He's not a controlling Master, He's a loving Father – and Jesus, who died for us, is sat with God in heaven, seeing us and cheering us on. He's with us: because of His love, nothing can be against us – not trouble or hardship or persecution, because in Him, we are more than conquerors.

God knew what He was doing when He made you. He put you in this place at this time, with these people; and He gave you your heart. He gave you the love you have for the things you love, He gave you your passion for the things you are passionate about. He made you so that you would see the injustices in the world like only you can see them, and He made you the way you are for a reason.

And if we are doing life with God on our side, then we are always in the majority. God has already said **'Yes' and 'Amen'** to all of the dreams that He has put on your heart; to pursue the purpose that God has given you in the world is to pursue Him. If He is for us then all of those dreams and ideas that He has put on your heart are in His hands: He is a generous Father who wants to give you all things.

In all these things, we are **more than conquerors** through Him who loves us; we are the hands and feet on earth of He who loves us, and He gives us the competence to get things done.

Questions for Reflection:

1. *In which areas of your life have you found yourself feeling incompetent in the past?*

2. *Is there anything in the stories of Joshua or Jeremiah that encourages you in this area?*

3. *What areas of strength and competence did God put in you when He created you?*

CHAPTER SEVEN
I AM NEEDED

"If I have a hope, it's that God sat over the dark nothing and wrote you and me, specifically, into the story and put us with the sunset and the rainstorm as though to say, Enjoy your place in my story. The beauty of it means you matter, and you can create within it even as I have created you"
– Donald Miller, A Million Miles in a Thousand Years

We know that we are not just slaves, passively here just to serve a Master; we know that we are children of God, living in an intimate relationship with our Father, who created us. So, if this is true, what does that mean for our lives, here on earth? As Christians, we believe that we're going to get to spend an eternity with our Father in heaven; but we have 90-odd years to live here on earth. The cool thing about a relationship with God is that He is not only interested in what happens when we die: He is concerned about who we are now, how we spend our time, what we are doing with our time here. He's interested in the kind of person that we are, how we choose to live, how we treat others. He loves it when we enjoy our day – he loves to see us happy, full of joy, full of love for the life that He has given us.

God loves to see us encouraging each other, spending time with each other, building friendships and families. He loves it when these relationships bring us joy; and boy, does God love to see us laugh. Your laugh brings so much joy to God, just as an earthly Father loves to see his children happy. Your life here, at this time, in the place that you are, is not a waste, and it's not an accident. Your story was designed, woven into God's story, with the sunsets and the rainstorms and the rest of God's creation: you are among the beauty of His creation. The beauty of it all means that you matter, and you can create among it, just as God has created you.

I wonder what images come to mind, when you think of living life to the full. Maybe the Instagram-worthy pictures: lying on beaches, getting to all the right parties, having all the good things in life.

Here's what Jesus says: *"The thief comes only to steal and kill and de-*

stroy; I have come that they may have life, and have it to the full." (John 10:10)

I'm not sure that Jesus was talking about parties when he said that He came so that we might have life to the full. Not that parties and beaches are wrong, necessarily; but if this is all we're aiming for, then we're seriously missing out. Because actually, following Jesus is one of the most exciting things. Following Jesus means freedom, joy, peace beyond measure.

This where God is asking us to find our strength. Not in how amazing we are, or the things that we can do, or the people that we hang out with, but in Him – being strong means admitting that we can't do it on our own, and knowing that we need a saviour. We can't have freedom without Jesus. Without Jesus we are slaves – slaves to sin, and we are living in darkness. But when we know Jesus, He sets us free, He covers us, and our strength does not come from ourselves, but from Him.

God Loves Creativity

Our God is a creative God – He created the world and everything in it. Our God is the God who made the sky that beautiful shade of blue on a sunny day; He made sunsets and rainbows. He dusted the top of the mountaintops with snow, He breathed the sky into creation and He loves it when we lie back on a dark night, amazed by His creation. He created every colour and shade and texture that we can imagine; He came up with the seasons and spoke them into existence.

We – all of us – are His little creative ones, made in His image, with His creative gene inside us. He loves when we create; when we use that creativity to make something that was not there before, in a way that only we could. He loves it when we use the things that we can do, the things that we can make, to bring joy and pleasure to His children; He loves when we use our skills and gifts and talents, and share them with other people. I get to sit in a coffee shop and doodle, and God loves this: just enjoying His presence, being so natural and comfortable with Him in all I do.

Do not tell me that you are not a creative person. You are human, you are made in His image, and you have His creativity inside of you. Creativity is such an ingrained part of our humanity that to keep moving forwards is to be creative. When we think through how to write an email, carefully form our words, His creativity is moving in us. When we sit and watch a video game, or a movie, or a TV show, and imagine ourselves as that main character; fighting the zombies, saving the princess, saving the world – it is

His creativity that makes our heart beat a little bit faster. He even understands the way we smile as we take that dish out of the oven, proud of what we have created, or step back and admire the freshly painted garden fence after a mornings' work. God loves your moments of creativity – this is the gift that He has given to you, and you using this gift brings Him so much joy. He loves it when we use our creativity in our lives, because our lives are not the place where we wait to go to heaven: they're the place that He has put us, and given us dreams and ideas and purpose. Our lives matter, and the way that we use our lives matters.

So be creative. Know that God has knit you into this story, with the sunsets and the rainstorms and the seasons and the mountaintops; He has put you here to enjoy His creation, and to create within it as He has created you. Use your place in His story – be an active contributor to this world. Use your words – say the things that other people need to hear. Create something beautiful that will capture the imagination of others. Make something that is delicious to taste, to bless the people that you love. Do not let this world wash over you, but claim your place in it and use your place to add something to the world.

"We are all in danger of thinking, 'Someday I shall be fulfilled. Someday I shall have the courage to start another life which will develop my talent', without ever considering the very practical use of that talent today in a way which will enrich other people's lives, develop the talent, and express the fact of being a creative creature." (Edith Schaeffer[7])

Purpose

So if we are here on purpose – if we have a place in God's creation and we the things that we do here are woven into a bigger story of God's kingdom – then the things that we do in this life matter.

The next part of this journey is to work out what it is that we are here for. Purposelessness is a terrible feeling. Unsure of what it is that we are doing, or why we're here, we just float – and then wonder what it is about ourselves that has got us into that place. Are we not good enough? Are we not trying hard enough? Are we not interested in the right things? But we have a purpose, simply by being the person that we are, in the place that we are, with a passion for the things that we have a passion for. The word "vo-

---

[7]Schaeffer, E., *'The Hidden Art of Homemaking'*

cation" – the word that we would use to describe our job or the things that we do – comes from the Latin word *"vocare",* meaning **"the work a person is called to by God." (Buechner[8])** To be called means that there must be someone who has called us – and for us, that means that we are called by God.

There are some things that we are all called to, and these things are the same for all who believe: we are called to faith in Jesus; we are called to the Kingdom of God; we are called to eternal life; and we are called to a life of obedience. These do not differ from person to person: if we have a relationship with the living God, these are the things that we are called to live in, and they are things that we will continue to be called to throughout our lives.

But beyond that, we each must decide what it is that we will spend our life doing, whether in work or in the way that we spend our time; and this is not the same for all believers. Some people are called to become leaders of the church; some are called to the secular business world. Some decide to dedicate their life to caring for old people, or young people, or people with disabilities, or children. Some become teachers, or police officers, or shop assistants, or cleaners. Some people are talented at singing, or dancing, or acting, or writing, and pursue a career in this, or are so passionate about it that it fills their life. There are some things that many share, but work within in different ways: family, community, work.

As a youth worker, one of the questions that I help young people work through the most is just this: *what am I doing with my life? What do I want to do? What should I do at university? What job do I want to do? What if I make the wrong choice?*

The idea of choosing the thing that we are going to do for the rest of our lives is hugely daunting. Or maybe we get to the place of feeling like we've made the wrong decision – bored of what we're doing, knowing that it isn't right for us but not knowing what the alternative is; not knowing where to go next. Our passions, skills and talents are so unique and individual, changing from person to person, that if we make these decisions based on the pressures that are put on us by society, or the things that the well-meaning people around us think we should be doing, we'll very quickly realise that our passions and our work don't match up.

---

[8] Buchner, F., *'Wishful Thinking: A Theological ABC'*

It's possible to go through life working just for the sake of working, and finding enjoyment in other things. But we are called to something better than this – work is such a fundamental part of who we are, and it is part of our calling from God: we are put here to be active participants in God's creation. A theologian called Alister McGrath wrote this: *"The work of believers is thus seen to possess a significance that goes far beyond the visible results of that work. It is the person working, as much as the resulting work, that is significant to God. There is no distinction between spiritual and temporal, sacred and secular work. All human work, however lowly, is capable of glorifying God. Work is, quite simply, an act of praise — a potentially productive act of praise. Work glorifies God, it serves the common good, and it is something through which human creativity can express itself."*

God is interested in the process. He's interested in you living out all that you were created to be, and work is a huge aspect of this: it's an act of praising God. It's part of taking our place in God's creation and working **with** God; not just being Sunday Christians, but letting our faith affect our whole life. Therefore, working through ideas of what it is that you want to do with your life is a conversation that happens between *you and God*. Everyone will have an opinion; input as to what it is that we should be doing. But ultimately, your life is an act of praise to God, and that praise needs to come from you.

Calling comes from an encounter with the living God. I'm not necessarily talking angels appearing and giving you specific instructions, or a banner across the sky telling you what it is that you should be doing; but it's a conversation with the God who made you, about what it is that He is asking you to do here. We know that we don't have to go far to have this conversation: God has given us His Spirit so that we can have an intimate relationship with Him, so all we have to do is be open to listening to that still, small voice that is available to all of us.

What's the easiest way to do this? Ask Him! God promises that we can *"ask and it will be given to you; seek and you will find; knock and the door will be opened to you." (Matthew 7:7)* We have a loving God, who wants to give us good things: He wants to give us all that we need and ask for in prayer. There are three "kinds" of prayer here. We can **ask** for the things that we need or desire, either in the physical, or the things that would add to our character, and our Father, the provider, promises to provide. We can seek – our efforts to find the things of God as we look to grow closer to our Father – and He promises that we will find the things that we are looking for. And we can knock, wanting to see our Father's face, and He promises that He will open the door for us. Working out our calling often involves each of these, stepping into that intimate relationship with our Father, seeking the things that we can participate in as part of His kingdom, and asking for the things that are needed as we walk out our calling in the world.

Power in Experience

Choosing the path that you want to take in life can be so difficult, and if you are between the ages of 16 and 25 and thinking about your options for the next part of your life, that decision can feel like it is loaded with so much pressure. We are often sold the tried-and-tested trodden path for most of our school career: you finish school, you go to sixth form, you get the grades that you need to go to university and then you choose the subject that makes the most sense based on your A-levels. You finish university, and you start a graduate scheme, or an internship, or work experience in the area that you want to go into. You get a graduate job and work your way up; saying the right things, doing things the right way, getting in with the right people until you work your way up the ladder. You're seen as successful if you're settled into a career within a year of graduating, and you'll probably be in that career for the next forty to fifty years.

For most of the population, jobs are the tool that provides us with the money that is needed for the rest of our lives: it allows us to travel to the places we want to go, to live in the place we want to live, to spend time with friends in the way that we want to, to eat and drink and be merry. We live in a society in which it isn't really possible to live without a solid income, so we become trapped in the vicious circle; you must earn enough to pay your rent, and you must pay your rent so you can continue to live and work.

There's got to be more to life than this right? More than living to work and working to live, more than doing the things that we do just because it is the logical path and the most likely to earn us a liveable income. What if we could have all the things that we need, and achieve all the things that we want to achieve, by taking a path that is less trodden?

Path A is the traditional education-scheme-job-promotion route; getting the right grades, moving on to the next thing and working our way up. But life doesn't come with only one option, despite what we are told: there are many options, and each carries worth depending on our motives and intent behind it.

There is a **Path B**. There are many things that university, graduate schemes and graduate-level jobs offer; but it may be the case that these things can be found outside the traditional route, in a way that will set you on a path that you are passionate about, and that produces real fruit in your life. Now, I'm speaking as a graduate with a BA in Youth and Community Work and Practical Theology from Gloucestershire University; it is not that university is never the right route. But, like in everything else in life, we have the power to think outside of the cultural norms that we grow up in; we have options and we are never on a set path that we cannot get out of. If going to university will bring you closer to the things that you want to achieve and the path you want to take, then that is absolutely the best thing for you to do; but if not, then your life is so much bigger than whether you have a degree or not.

Here are some of the components that a university education will offer you, and some alternative routes that you can take to these areas:

- **Time to practice your skills, and have a go:** A university education is broken down into modules and topics; teaching you the theory and skills that are relevant to that area, and then testing you in the form of an essay, presentation or an exam. If you choose a creative degree, coursework and practical assessment will give you the opportunity to show what you can do, and to put those skills into your work. If you choose not to go to university, you can find this by taking up other learning opportunities or finding people who will teach you these skills. You'll also learn through practical experience, and learning on the job is a very valid route. Although you don't come out with a certificate at the other end, the product of your work will be the evidence that you can achieve the goals in that area.

- **Contacts and community**: University is great, because you spend three years or more in a group of people who are passionate about the same things as you, and are likely to end up in the same kind of career as you. As well as getting you through the university experience, these relationships can turn into valuable contacts for your professional career. The community means that when you're struggling, demotivated or underachieving, you have a safety net of people who are on the same page as you and who support each other in the low moments. Outside of university, this community may be found in networking and time spent co-working on projects that are not your own – even voluntarily – to find passionate people that are on the same path as you. It means finding community outside of the work environment; networks of family and friends who understand your passion and your vision, and who are cheering you on. It means inviting others along on projects, and partnering with people, so that your work is not simply the product of one mind. Although these relationships will need to be more intentional than relationships formed in a university environment, you really get to choose who you want to spend your time with.

- **Inspiration:** University helps you to try out a wide range of topics and experiences, and to find the things that make your heart beat a little faster. It might be that you can go on to specialise in that area in the last year of your degree or in another course; or it might be that this passion leads you into a career that you love. There's time to dabble and learn a little bit about a lot of things – there's time to find experience outside of lectures and to find out where your skills lie. You'll meet lecturers and tutors that give you a fire in your heart for their subject and encourage you to take it further. You can spend time around people who are passionate about the same things, and try projects together. On an alternative route, inspiration comes from trying lots of different things and finding out what you are passionate about; it comes from listening to people who are doing the things that you want to do, and letting their thoughts and ideas inspire yours. It means immersing yourself in culture and listening to the ideas that emerge from your heart.

Education is important, and university is a completely valid life choice. But it is just that – a choice. We are not on a set path that we cannot divert from – we have the power to choose where we are going to put ourselves in life. It is our responsibility to learn, to engage with the world around us, and to be active participants in this world.

These words are from the rapper Tupac, speaking about education in 1988:

"School is really important: reading, writing, arithmetic. But what they tend to do is teach you reading, writing, arithmetic... and then teach you reading, writing, arithmetic again. Then again, then again, just making it harder and harder just to keep you busy. And that's where I think they messed up. There should be a class on drugs. There should be a class on sex education. No, real sex education, not just pictures and illogical terms. There should be a class on religious cults, there should be a class on police brutality, there should be a class on apartheid, there should be a class on racism in America, there should be a class on why people are hungry, but there's not, there's a class on... gym."

How different would our world be if every teenager had to take a class on why people were hungry? How much would a class on racism or police brutality affect the minds of the young people who are going to be the future leaders in our world? Whether we choose to go down the route of traditional education or not, we have a responsibility to be active participants, and to educate ourselves about the needs of the world. Education, whether it's provided by schooling or life experience, needs to help us to look at the world around us with a critical-thinking approach, and to imagine the world that we could live in, giving us the skills we need to participate in the change needed.

And when we are participating – when we are adding something to the world that we live in – our perceptions and ideas and the unique background and experience that we bring to these things changes them. We are needed to change the way that our world teaches young people about sex and relationships. We are needed to bring hope and equality into a world where racism, sexism, classism and gender inequality are rife. We are needed to bring a voice of clarity into a confused world.

When I left secondary school, I flipped through the college prospectus with no idea of what I wanted to do, and, seeing a picture of a puppy, signed up to do a BTEC in Animal Management – the equivalent of four A-levels. Spending two years doing this showed me, although it mainly involved spending my days hanging out with cool animals, it wasn't what I wanted to do for the rest of my life. I grew up knowing that I wouldn't go to university – by the time I finished sixth form, students were paying £6000 per year of university in the United Kingdom, and this seemed set to rise; a lot of money to throw away when I didn't know what I wanted to do.

At the same time, I had become a Christian and got involved in my local church; mainly sitting in the aisles with the children, racing toy cars up and down with them and spinning them around in circles. I was seventeen and found that the youth group was an easy place to be, helping to lead small groups and talking to the other teenagers. So, when an application for a youth work internship landed on my lap, it didn't seem a million miles away from what I should be doing.

I moved my Vauxhall-Corsa-boot-full of things up to Northamptonshire, trained for a year, working at a parish church, and absolutely fell in love with youth work. I was spending my days helping people through some of the toughest times; comforting, helping, guiding. I was writing sessions and programmes and teaching young people about relationship with God. I was working in the community, in programmes that were making a real difference in people's lives. After a year, I'd decided that youth work was the path I wanted to explore; and annoyingly, I was pointed towards a degree in Cambridge.

Deciding to do the degree is one of the best decisions that I've made to date. I was training in something that I knew I'd been called to do, learning about adolescent development and theology and pastoral care and diversity, and how the whole lot fitted together into one big picture. University gave me a language and a context for the calling that I had on my life.

Education was about giving me a passion about issues that I saw around me so that I could make a difference; giving me a language and skills to be able to work to fix these issues, and giving me the time to practice things, make mistakes, and learn where my skills fitted best. I'm now working as a youth worker in Cambridge, and although university was a part of that journey, it was also part of my story, along with the community that formed around me in Cambridge: a story of life experience, mistakes made, training from other places, inspiring people and a bigger calling on my life.

Remember: whatever life looks like, you have the power to change it. You are not stuck. You are not trapped in one career just because that is what you chose to do when you were seventeen. We always have the power to turn our life in a completely different direction, and go after the things that we are called to do.

Your Passions, and the Worlds' Greatest Needs

Passion and purpose go hand in hand, I've found. I feel like the things that I am doing have purpose when I enjoy what I am doing, and when I can see the things that I am doing producing fruit and making a difference. For us to feel successful in whatever role we have, these factors need to be present: some kind of enjoyment or fulfilment from the job, and some kind of result from the work that we are doing. These factors can be found in every job and role – but if the role that we are in does not match our character, passions, skills and talents, one or both of these will be missing.

"The place God calls you to is the place where your deep gladness and the world's deep hunger meet" (Buechner[9])

I love these words from Buechner; we find our purpose, the place that God is calling us to, where our deep gladness – our passions, gifts, talents, personality and dreams – meet the needs that we see in the world. Where these two meet, a job stops being a job, and becomes our purpose. We are

---

[9] Beuchner, F., *'Wishful Thinking: A Theological ABC'*

there, in that moment, to do that particular thing, because we bring the passions and skills that are needed to get it done. Where these two meet, we have a significance that goes far beyond the job – we are a part of God's story, actively participating in His kingdom.

Our calling is not the same thing as selfish ambition, or self-interest: it's found much deeper – it's something that is a part of who you are, and who you were created to be. God put this inside you for a reason. The goal is not happiness and self-fulfilment, but a life that makes a difference and contributes to God's story.

The Venn Diagram

Let's have a go at this together; I love a Venn diagram. Grab a piece of paper, or your journal, or a spare page in this book, and a pen, and you're going to need to draw two circles that overlap in the middle – hopefully, something that looks a little bit like this:

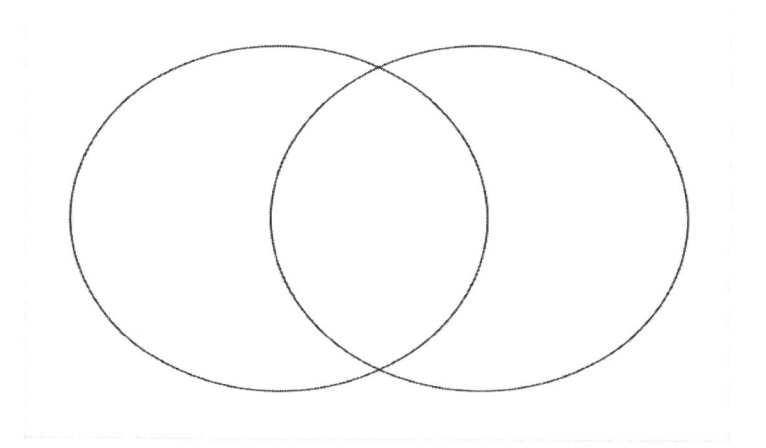

The left-hand circle represents **you** – all of the things that we've thought about throughout this journey. It's your talents, skills, dreams, passions, and the visions that you have. Listen to your life – what is it that makes you who you are? Listen to your life in the exciting moments and the monotony, in the peaks and the valleys. Pay attention to these moments, because they reveal things about us that were put inside us, by God, for a purpose. These things are whispering about the kind of work that God has given us to do.

Now, moving on to the right-hand circle. This one is all about **the world** – it's the need you see, the people around you. What's going on in the world? What's going on in your town, or with the people around you? Maybe there's a particular issue that sticks out with you, or a place, or a group of people. Take a while and ask God – what it is that He's put on your heart?

When Beuchner was first describing this idea, he suggested that the way to listen to your life, to see what it is that God has put on your heart, is to follow your feet: *"when you wake in the morning, called by God to be a self again, if you want to know who you are, watch your feet. Because where your feet take you, that is who you are".* This part of the picture might involve the things that we want to spend our time doing and the people that we want to spend our time with. It might involve the things that we take extra care to notice as we walk past in the street, or the issues that we spend some time and effort researching and getting involved in.

The middle of the diagram is where the gold lies. This picture is totally unique: God has made you, like no other person, with these skills and passions and dreams inside you, and then put you in a place where you would see these things around you; He's given you a heart that would pick up on these people or those issues. Where these two meet is where we can start to find purpose: this is the journey that we all continue on for the rest of our lives. This is not a one-size-fits-all, tick the box answer that will give you the solution that you need – but it can help us to focus our priorities and our time to the things that God has put on our hearts.

You are so needed on this earth. The danger is that we might get stuck in what we can't do, feeling weak or wondering why God is not working through us. But we are free from the law that determines whether we are right with God or not based on our performance. Instead, we get to be a part of this amazing co-mission with God: it is not our mission, our job, our calling, but His. Everything comes from Him, and we are called to be active participants in His Kingdom. God's mission began the moment He said "let there be light"; the whole of this earth is full of the glory of God, and we have the honour of living and working in that light.

Questions for Reflection:

1. *Are you creative? Where does this creativity manifest in your life?*

2. *Have a go at filling in the venn diagram for yourself: the left side being the strengths and talents that God has put in you, and the right side being the need that you see in the world.*

3. *Where do the two meet?*

CHAPTER EIGHT
I AM KIND

We know that we are made in the image of God: we are created, we're loved, and we are children of the God who created us. We've looked at our gifts, our purpose, the reason that we're here, and we've thought about what it is that makes us unique. We've learnt what God says about us, and decided to believe the truth, rather than what the world says about us. But this isn't the end of the story; it's not supposed to be all about us. We fit into a bigger picture, and we are not designed to live a life of isolation. We're constantly interacting with other people, all day, every day. Our lives are spent in community with other people – we don't just do life on our own.

Our generation is known as the lovers of social media; the ones who are always on our phones. I really love my phone – unashamedly. I love Instagram, I love Snapchat, I love Facebook. When I'm doing it well, it makes me feel more connected to the people around me; it's a really quick, easy way to check in with my friends. But Snapchat doesn't have anything on a Friday night in with some girlfriends: blankets, terrible movie on, chocolate ice cream in full flow. It doesn't have anything on sitting in a coffee shop with someone I love, hearing all about their adventures. It doesn't have anything on a comforting hug with someone who's struggling, being able to be there and be present when times get tough.

We're not made to do life by ourselves – we're meant to have people around us. When God made Adam and Eve, the first people, He made Adam and then He said this: ***"it is not good for man to be alone. I will make a helper suitable for him"***. The word for helper in the Bible means partner, a "second self". Someone to do life with, ready to comfort, ready to help – someone on your team. This is how we're supposed to be living life, together – not just with our romantic partners, but in every relationship. We're made to live life in community.

And that's hard sometimes – it's much easier to feel like we're connected because people are "liking" what we're doing on Facebook, because we can make our lives look amazing online. It's very tempting to try to manufacture an incredible life on Facebook, because then the walls are up, and no-one has to see the real you.

Social media is a great aid, but cannot be a substitute for real relationships with real people. Our Facebook profile can be a fantastic way for our friends and the people around us to connect with us, to check in, share photos and moments with us; but these need to be expansions of the connections that we have with people in real life. When we only live in a world of social media, our world becomes foggy with thousands of voices; photos of babies that we will never meet, weddings that we have no care to go to, thoughts and opinions that cloud our thinking and make our world much busier. We feel a responsibility to keep up with this mass of voices – for the sake of networking, or politeness, or nosiness, wondering whether other people's lives are better than ours – but instead we become hyperconnected, trying so hard to keep up with the mass of voices that we fail to be there for the few voices that really matter.

Relationships are not always easy. They're not always instant. We cannot neglect them for months, and then "like" something and pick up where we left off, not in real life. But we were never designed to do life on our own; we were made to live in community.

Therefore if you have any encouragement from being united with Christ, if any comfort from his love, if any common sharing in the Spirit, if any tenderness and compassion, then make my joy complete by being like-minded, having the same love, being one in spirit and of one mind. Do nothing out of selfish ambition or vain conceit. Rather, in humility value others above yourselves, not looking to your own interests but each of you to the interests of the others. (Philippians 2:1-4)

If we are united with Christ, we are also united with each other, because we share in one Spirit – we are eternally connected to each other as the body of Christ. This is how we should live, then: being like-minded, having the same love, doing nothing out of selfish ambition for ourselves but valuing others above ourselves. This is a tough challenge for us as believers, and one that does not come naturally in our current culture: a culture that tells us to go after the things that we want, to use networks and social media to help ourselves, to make ourselves more popular and give ourselves a leg-up. Instead, we're told to look at others as above ourselves, not connecting in a shallow way, but sharing in the same spirit and having the same love. The comfort that we receive from sharing in the same Spirit as Christ should be the same comfort that we give to others by sharing in the same love.

Love does not look like "likes". It does not look like checking in once in a while. It looks like sharing life, sharing stories, rejoicing together, mourning together. It means comforting with the same love that Christ comforts us. Let's use social media in a way that allows us to do that; not that pulls us away from the people that need us to invest in them the most.

The good news is that we do not need to worry about this in our own strength: it's not about making yourself into the perfect person so that you are able to love others. Like capability, strength, courage and boldness, there are some characteristics that we will show if we have the Spirit of God inside of us; fruits of the Spirit. Just as fruit will grow if a seed is planted and nurtured, fruit will be evident in our character if we have the Holy Spirit planted in us.

But the fruit of the Spirit is love, joy, peace, patience, kindness, goodness, faithfulness, gentleness and self control. (Galatians 5:22-23, ESV)

With God living through us, these are the characteristics that will overflow out of us; not manufactured by us, but in us by design, from our designer. We are flawed, we are human, and we won't have all of these, in full, all the time, but this is good news – the Word says that if we ask our Dad for something, we'll be given it! We can ask Him to help make us more patient, more kind, more loving; it isn't about striving to be those things, but Him growing these things in us.

Kindness

Kindness comes from knowing our identity – as God's chosen people, these are the things that we should walk in. Knowing who we are means knowing who others are too. If we are children of God, then everyone else is too – and there is a humility in treating others with the same kindness and compassion as you would like to be treated.

Therefore, as God's chosen people, holy and dearly loved, clothe yourselves with compassion, kindness, humility, gentleness and patience. (Colossians 3:12)

Note that this does not say "these are the things you should do"; it says "these are the things we should clothe ourselves in" – this is much less about what we do, and much more about the character and values that we put on. If kindness is something we value, something that we "put on" every day, then we are going to treat the people around us with kindness: but if kindness is something that we try to do in our own strength, we're going to fall down very quickly when we come up against someone who is difficult to be kind to.

> ***Be kind and compassionate to one another, forgiving each other, just as in Christ God forgave you. (Ephesians 4:32)***

We're not talking about hollow-hearted politeness based on the way that we feel we should act; but kindness that comes from the love and compassion that God has for us. The way we treat people should be an overflow of the love that God has for us – there's no point in doing this out of works; that is not real love. Instead, we should be living in a way that means people see something of God's love in us, through the way that we love others.

Not Always Easy

All of this sounds wonderful on the surface; but, as we know, loving others is not always easy, and fluffy, and nice. When I talk about kindness, I'm not talking about fluffy, surface-level politeness for the people who make it easy for us to love them.

Kindness means speaking up for the people who don't have a voice. It means going the extra mile for the people who wouldn't go the extra inch for us. It means putting one foot in front of the other and doing the things for people that nobody else is doing. It means seeing a child of God, when they are making every effort to make the world hate them. In most cases, I've found, the people who are the most difficult to love are the people most in need of love and compassion. Kindness is love with work boots on.

This is who our God is: *"**He upholds the cause of the oppressed and gives food to the hungry. The Lord sets prisoners free, the Lord gives sight to the blind, the Lord lifts up those who are bowed down, the Lord loves the righteous. The Lord watches over the foreigner and sustains the fatherless and the widow, but he frustrates the ways of the wicked. (Psalm 146:7-9)***

Humans have so much value to God, because He is their creator, and He loves them. The human personality has so much value in His sight, and that is not simply limited to the ones who hold value in our sight, but all: the widow and the orphan, the refugee, the gay, the needy, the broken, the ones that don't come to us in a neat package. The widow and the orphan especially seem to be taken under God's care, from the days of Moses, and the responsibility was given to the righteous – us – to care for them. The

Lord *sustains*; He sees them in their pain and their brokenness, and He gives them the strength to carry on when they don't feel like they can do it by themselves. He watches over people, He sets people free, He lifts people up and He gives them exactly what they need. And while all of this comes from God, we are His hands and legs on the earth. We are the ones who can bend down to talk to the ones in need; we can feed the hungry; we can lay hands on the sick and expect God to do great works through us. We can put our work boots on and go out and love the ones that God is asking us to love; not with nice, fluffy politeness, but real love that changes lives.

"Do not deprive the foreigner or the fatherless of justice, or take the cloak of the widow of the pledge." (Deuteronomy 24:17) God was speaking a radical new voice into a world where these people were seen as "less than"; but I'm not sure He would be saying anything different in today's culture.

God cares about the people that society doesn't, and all through the Bible we see Him treating people with a radical love that was completely new in that culture. In the Church, if we are marginalising the same people that the world pushes out, then we've got a huge problem. We speak of how all lives are created equally by God, and yet this is not echoed in the way that we treat the widow and the orphan, or the refugees, or the ones that act and live in a way that is different from us.

This is who our God is:

The Lord builds up Jerusalem; he gathers the exiles of Israel. He heals the brokenhearted and binds up their wounds. He determines the number of the stars and calls them each by name. (Psalm 147:2-4)

He does it; not us. He doesn't expect us to sort ourselves out. I love the contrast here between the big picture and the small picture: the same God who binds up the wounds of the brokenhearted knows the number of stars in the sky, because He breathed them into creation. Let's not doubt that He who knows everything there is to know about the universe also knows our hearts, and cares for us enough to take care of us when we are brokenhearted.

We have a freedom that comes from knowing our Saviour, and yet we feel that we have the right to keep this freedom from those that we deem unacceptable. Whether they are refugees, women going through abortions, rape victims, those from races and cultures other than our own, or people who identify with a different sexuality or gender identity to us: we treat them differently, we do not treat them with the same kindness as our peers, because ultimately, we are uncomfortable. They don't fit into our nice, neat box. They might reject us. But they are still God's creation, still humans who deserve the same dignity and kindness as anyone else. Love is not always easy.

We're in a world where we are regularly grieving the tragedy of mass shootings; terrorism, humans killing other humans. Over the few years before this book was written, the world has mourned schoolchildren, military personnel, movie-goers, huge crowds in Paris. It's easy to feel hopeless, even numb to the news; the temptation is to jump in to conversations about gun laws and immigration, and dive into the sea of discussion and debate on social media. But before all of that, this is a tragedy. God is grieving with us, and these were human beings with dignity and value.

Romans reminds us to get alongside those who are hurting: ***"Rejoice with those who rejoice; mourn with those who mourn." (Romans 12:15)*** Before anything else, our priority should be with people: praying with people, supporting people, loving people. Kindness is love with work boots on.

Forgiveness

Here we go; deep breath. This is the subject that can be the most difficult to talk about, but it is also the thing that can most get in the way of us living out all that we are meant to be in God. Love is not easy. Everything God asks us to do is counter-cultural; the natural response is to stay angry, to hold on to grudges, to allow ourselves to feel hurt. But God calls us to act differently:

> ***Now instead, you ought to forgive and comfort him, so that he will not be overwhelmed by excessive sorrow. I urge you, therefore, to reaffirm your love for him. Another reason I wrote to you was to see if you would stand the test and be obedient in everything. Anyone you forgive, I also forgive. And what I have forgiven – if there was anything to forgive – I have forgiven in the sight of Christ for your sake, in order that Satan might not outwit us. For we are not unaware of his schemes. (2 Corinthians 2:7-11)***

When things are going well, friendships and relationships are so good for our heart. We feel like our friends could never do anything wrong, we feel connected, we want to spend time with people because we like them!

But when things go wrong, we react out of a need to protect ourselves and protect our hearts. Everything in us does not want to forgive them – we want to remain angry with them, and to be offended by the things that they do.

When we accept Christ, and even more when we get to know His grace, we give up the right to be offended. We are not living for ourselves any more, but for Him; and from now on we perceive no-one from a worldly point of view, because we are all children of God. So how can we hold an offence against another, who is on the same page as us?

"Now instead, you ought to forgive and comfort him…"; we need each other on team, and when we hold unforgiveness against another, we are not on their side. We are to forgive freely, fully and liberally. The choice as to whether or not to forgive has been taken away from us: *"Be kind and compassionate to one another, forgiving each other, just as in Christ God forgave you." (Ephesians 4:32)* We have no right to hold on to this hurt, because Christ has already taken it from us.

"I urge you, therefore, to reaffirm your love for him…"; God is already in the situation, He knows everything that is going on, and He is our helper. We can ask for God's help to approach situations with kindness and wisdom, and an ability to reaffirm our love, while helping others to understand all that they need to understand.

"The reason I wrote to you was to see if you would stand the test and be obedient in everything…"; my obedience in forgiving is not based on works – on just doing what is right. Instead, obedience flows from belonging to Christ: *"we received grace and apostleship to call all the Gentiles to the obedience that comes from faith." (Romans 1:5)* My obedience is not based on belonging to the church, or on having to do the right thing; but on belonging to Jesus, and His love flowing from me.

"In order that Satan might not outwit us"; Satan is the *accuser.* He has plans and schemes to mess up all that is good. When there are relationships that are good, he will be against them; and when we hold on to unforgiveness, we are looking away from God and looking at ourselves – just what Satan wants! But Satan doesn't have any power here – he is just the accuser. All he can do is sow doubts and questions and lies, to try and hold us in a place of bitterness. We can choose to break this cycle, and he has no power to fight against us when he is told to leave.

"And what I have forgiven – if there was anything to forgive – I have forgiven in the sight of Christ for your sake, in order that Satan might not outwit us. For we are not unaware of his schemes". We have the choice to forgive and move on because, just as we are a child of God, so are they, and together we can do awesome things for the Kingdom.

But sometimes hurt is deep, and offences are serious, and it is not a case of just rebuilding a relationship and working together. Sometimes we would be putting ourselves in danger if we did that. I don't want to minimise your suffering: humans are capable of terrible things and hurt can go really deep.

But the **truth** is the Jesus is that the *"God of all comfort, who comforts us in all our troubles, so that we can comfort those in any trouble with the comfort we ourselves receive from God." (2 Corinthians 1:4)* Our comfort does not come from others treating us in the right way, but from God.

"But this happened that we might not rely on ourselves, but on God, who raises the dead"; we will get hurt, and people have the potential to break us. But when these things happen, we have the choice to look to an all-powerful God – who raises the dead and therefore absolutely has the power to raise us out of the hurt that we are feeling, and into joy.

I encourage you to use the questions at the end of this chapter to begin to work through some of the things in your life that you are holding on to. Grab a cup of tea, deep breath, and here we go:

Questions for Reflection:

1. *Are there any trials or circumstances that have been on your mind as you read this chapter?*

2. *In these circumstances, how much has your heart been surrendered to God?*

3. *Is it hard to believe that God can fully heal you in this area? Why?*

4. *What would forgiveness look like for you in your life, right now?*

CHAPTER NINE
I AM POSSIBLE

I love those words of Neith Boyce – the Vogue columnist from the 1890s, who wrote a piece called the "Girl Bachelor", claiming that she was trying to "convince the world that she was possible". Neith lived in a way that was drastically different from the rest of her generation, and she used her voice and her place in the world to encourage others to do the same. She was a girl who was capable of doing her own thing in a world that told her that she needed to be dependent on another, and she wouldn't settle for the labels that were put on her: ***"I shall never be an old maid, for I have elected to be a Girl Bachelor,"*** she said. She claimed the right to define her own place in the world, and to thrive in that place.

As children of God, this is ultimately what we are called to do: to live in a way that differs drastically from the rest of our generation, and to refuse to sit under the labels that the world wants to put on us. We are called to shake off the stereotypes that have been put on us by the expectations of others; asked to take captive every thought and only choose to keep the ones that contain the truth about who we are. We are called to know that we are a new creation, hidden in Him, and to live out of this: shaking off our old selves and accepting the truth of who we are. We are called to live in this crazy, ridiculous, abounding love story with our Father; knowing how loved we are, and having this love overflow from us so much that it is evident to the people around us. We are called to be comfortable in our own skin; comfortable with the lumps and the bumps, comfortable with not looking like the idealised picture that the world expects us to live up to. We are called to find our strength in Him; to look at the truth of who we are in faith, rather than believe our perception of reality. We are called to live in the competence that comes from God; to be strong and courageous, for tomorrow the Lord will do great things among us. We are called to use our place in God's creation; creatively, deliberately, purposefully using our voice to bring glory to our Father. We are called to look at the world around us with heavenly eyes, and see the wonder and fresh mercy that there is in every day.

Worry

But all of this is so different from the way that most of the world is living. Choosing to live for Jesus instead of for the approval of others is just about the most radical thing you can do. In a world that tells us that we need to sort our own lives out and go after our own destinies, we have a truth that is crazily, radically different:

So do not worry, saying, 'What shall we eat?' or 'What shall we drink?' or 'What shall we wear?' For the pagans run after all these things, and your heavenly Father knows that you need them. But seek first his kingdom and his righteousness, and all these things will be given to you as well. (Matthew 6:31-33)

Jesus is warning His disciples against getting distracted by the day-to-day worries of life; what to eat, what to drink, what to wear. These things make us lose sight of God and make us look to ourselves. The need to worry about these things of daily life can cause the regular folk to live in just as much bondage as a love of money does for the rich. They are temporary things, and we do not need to worry about the comforts of this life, because we can leave it to God to handle it, knowing that He has a better plan for us. God knows that we need these things, and He loves us as a perfect Father, so He makes us a promise; if we look to Him first and live in His righteousness, all of the things that we need will be provided for us.

We are called to be assured and confident that God is our provider, and that He will therefore provide all that we need; to put our trust in Him and to know that He has got our backs. This is when we get the privilege of helping people through tough times, of praying with people in need, of seeing people inspired and full of joy, of sitting down and getting to hear awesome stories of their adventure, and of achieving great things for the Kingdom; because we are not looking at ourselves and our own needs, but at God and His creation. The *"best preservation is to commit ourselves to God's keeping" (Barnes)* – when we choose to trust in God, we don't need to go anywhere else, or rely on anything else for protection; because nothing else compares.

Therefore do not worry about tomorrow, for tomorrow will worry about itself. Each day has enough trouble of its own. (Matthew 6:34)

Worry has become an integral part of life for most of the world. For many people, it is so important that once old worries are gone and out of the way, they are almost intentionally seeking out new worries; it's a strange feeling to not having anything to worry about, and it can feel like we're not trying hard enough. Worry can become a lens through which we view the world, and without it we can struggle to find the meaning in life. The world tells you that there is plenty to be worried about: economic stress, political stress, personal finances, threats of terrorism and rogue nuclear nations; it would be considered odd if we weren't worried about the state of our world.

But we are called not to worry, but to have hope: do not worry about tomorrow, because tomorrow will happily worry about itself. Worrying will not add anything to a situation; it's a passive, pointless cycle that won't get us anywhere. We get to make a decision to live differently: ***"as for me, I will always have hope, I will praise you more and more." (Psalm 71:14)*** May today be an "as for me" marker for you. As for me, I will not worry, but will trust in God. As for me, I will choose not to believe this lie about myself, but choose to live in this truth.

May today be a day when you show the world that you are possible; that it is possible to know that you know that you know that what God says about you is true, and that there is a better alternative than bending to what the world says about you.

Isaiah Called

In Isaiah 6, we get to see the calling of an awesome prophet called Isaiah (funny that!). Up until chapter six, we'd had a glimpse of the state of the people of Israel, the children that God loved: God created them, He gave them life, but they had decided to turn away and try to do life their own way, and it led to total destruction and brokenness. The story seemed so hopeless, but there was hope in the ruins: out of it, God found Isaiah, called him to change the world around him, and used him to put things right. Isaiah was part of the people who had turned away, but God pulled him out and used him to speak into his generation.

This call from God came to Isaiah in a vision, as we read in Isaiah 6:

In the year that King Uzziah died, I saw the Master sitting on a throne — high, exalted! — and the train of his robes filled the Temple. Angel-seraphs hovered above him, each with six wings. With two wings they covered their faces, with two their feet, and with two they flew. And they called back and forth one to the other, Holy, Holy, Holy is GOD-of-the-Angel-

Armies. His bright glory fills the whole earth.

The foundations trembled at the sound of the angel voices, and then the whole house filled with smoke. (Isaiah 6:1-4, MSG)

Isaiah was part of his generation; he was one of the people who had turned away from God and done their own thing. The things that God was about to ask him to do couldn't be done in his own strength – he needed a call and an encounter with God. He saw God as He is – high on a throne, exalted, with angels hovering around Him singing His praise. His glory and beauty filled the earth, and I bet Isaiah was pretty stunned by what he saw.

This vision came to Isaiah in the year that the king of their land died – with that loss, God brought a vision for something new. So it is with all of our losses and all of our pain – God does not cause loss, but He uses our disappointments to turn us around and have us look at Him, as the enthroned God. While we are mourning the old, He gives us the hope to look at something new. Here, when the king died, Isaiah and the people of the land had the opportunity to see the King who had been hidden from them; when Uzziah died, the King became visible. Sometimes, God needs to take away whatever is in the way for us to see clearly.

Isaiah needed to see how glorious God is, in order for him to turn to Him and do all that he had been called to do.

I said, "Doom! It's Doomsday! I'm as good as dead! Every word I've ever spoken is tainted – blasphemous even! And the people I live with talk the same way, using words that corrupt and desecrate. And here I've looked God in the face! The King! GOD-of-the-Angel-Armies!"

Then one of the angel-seraphs flew to me. He held a live coal that he had taken with tongs from the altar. He touched my mouth with the coal and said, "Look. This coal has touched your lips. Gone your guilt, your sins wiped out." And then I heard the voice of the Master: "Whom shall I send? Who will go for us?"
I spoke up, "I'll go. Send me!" (Isaiah 6:5-8, MSG)

God completely cleansed Isaiah from the place of brokenness that he was in. While Isaiah's response was to beg for forgiveness from God and to feel guilt and shame for the things that he had done, God touched his lips and told him that it was all gone – his guilt, his sin, his shame.

The world works on the principles of guilt and restoration – having to say sorry and beg for forgiveness for the things that we do; having to *feel* sorry to be worthy of the restored relationship. But God only gives: forgiveness, wholeness, redemption.

God showed up for Isaiah in His glory, and when Isaiah's response was to grovel and beg for forgiveness, God took all of that off him, and instead called him into a bigger picture. This is exactly what He does for us. If you let Him, He'll take guilt; take sin, shame, sickness, worries and fears. Instead of us having to work to earn His love, He takes the things that harm us for free, and only gives us things that bless us.

He said, "Go and tell this people: "Listen hard, but you aren't going to get it; look hard, but you won't catch on. Make these people blockheads, with fingers in their ears and blindfolds on their eyes, so they won't see a thing, won't hear a word, so they won't have a clue about what's going on and, yes, so they won't turn around and be made whole."

Astonished, I said, "And Master, how long is this to go on?"
He said, "Until the cities are emptied out, not a soul left in the cities— Houses empty of people, countryside empty of people. Until I, GOD, get rid of everyone, sending them off, the land totally empty. And even if some should survive, say a tenth, the devastation will start up again. The country will look like pine and oak forest with every tree cut down— Every tree a stump, a huge field of stumps. But there's a holy seed in those stumps." (Isaiah 6:10-13, MSG)

God met Isaiah in his brokenness, pulled him out and gave him a vision that was much bigger and better. He told him that he was worthy of working for God's glory, even when he felt worthless. To us, broken things are worthless – only good for being thrown away – but God can take the broken things and make them into something better, that can be used for His glory. In a second, God took a broken person, made him whole and used him for His glory; it wasn't a long process of grovelling and self-improvement.

Made Whole

Without the broken body of Jesus, we cannot be made whole; but God saw that His people were broken and hurting, and He gave the ultimate sacrifice to bring wholeness and redemption. Broken people are the result of sin; but God sent His son, who was without sin, to be broken so that we might be whole. On the night before He died, Jesus broke the bread and said: *"this is my body, broken for you"*. We couldn't fix ourselves, but Jesus died that we might be made whole, and worthy of God's purpose.

The world tells us that if we are broken, then we need to live as a broken person: that we should know our place, and not try to reach for the sky when we should be in a heap on the ground. But we have a God who has healed us, who has forgiven us and made us whole in Him. You are not broken.

If you are not feeling whole and complete right now, here's a hug from us. Have a cup of tea – the well-known cure to any of life's issues - and take a breather. Spend some time with friends who understand what you're going through, and who are going to encourage you. And know that the things that you are going through do not define you as a person; you have so much ahead of you, and this is only the beginning. You can make the decision to put the truth of what God says about you over your perception of your life. It may feel like today is making or breaking your future, but the truth is that you have the most incredible future ahead of you. You are a child of God, your Dad is the coolest Dad of all Dads – He's got your name written on His hand. You are going to live a great life, full of amazing moments that you cannot even imagine yet.

The Word says that we are not broken, but righteous:

But now apart from the law the righteousness from God has been made known, to which the Law and the Prophets testify. This righteousness is given through faith in Jesus Christ to all who believe. (Romans 3:21-22)

No-one will ever be declared righteous by obeying the law and doing all the right things; but now we are seen as righteous through faith in Jesus Christ. The point of the law – the rules that the people lived by before Jesus – was not to make people perfect, but to make people conscious of their sin. Now, we are liberated from the law, and know that we are seen as perfect through Jesus. The point is not to observe the law to live up to God's expectations, but to know that we need Jesus because we cannot live up to God's standards.

And this righteousness is free to **all** who believe – it's a free gift, from God directly to you; and once you have it, you have it – that's it! It's been done, and is always available to us.

There is no difference between Jew and Gentile – for all have sinned and fall short of the glory of God, and are justified freely by his grace through the redemption that came by Jesus Christ. (Romans 3:22-24)

The first part of this verse is often preached in association with the things that we are doing wrong, pointing us towards guilt and shame: it says that none of us are good enough to live up to God's standards. But, rather than guilt and shame, this verse is surrounded by the truth of God's grace for us – we have fallen short, **and we are justified freely by grace**, which comes with faith in Jesus. We need this grace because we have fallen short, but His grace is freely given to us, so that we do not need to live in guilt and shame.

Where then, is boasting? It is excluded. Because of what law? The law that requires works? No, because of the law that requires faith.   (Romans 3:27)

I have no right to boast about how good I am, because I am not – it is His goodness in me. Instead, I can boast about all that He has done, to bring glory to Him. This is what a testimony should be: not *"look how good I am now;"* but *"look how good He is!"* – giving the world something to rejoice in.

It is counter-cultural, but completely possible, to live in a place of complete wholeness, of complete satisfaction with who we are and where we are at. It's completely possible to be thankful for all that God has done in our life, rather than letting ourselves feel broken by the things that are happening to us. If we know that the inside of us is good, and we know who we are, who created us, and what we're here for, this is going to come out in the way that we live, the passions that we have, and our friendships and relationships. As Roald Dahl said: *"if you have good thoughts, they will shine out of you like sunbeams, and you will always look lovely"*.

Protecting your heart does not mean putting up walls and not letting anyone near you; which our culture tells us to do. Instead, it means making sure the things that are inside you are good, because that is what will shine out of you. In Philippians, Paul writes this:

Whatever is true, whatever is noble, whatever is right, whatever is pure, whatever is lovely, whatever is admirable – if anything is excellent or praiseworthy – think about such things. (Philippians 4:8)

To protect your heart is to make an intentional decision to focus on the good rather than the bad. If you only think about what you do not have, you give the world a foothold to get in and tell you how you do not measure up to the people you're comparing yourself to. But we can make the choice to protect ourselves by deciding to believe the truth of God, and focus on the things that are right, and pure, and lovely.

<u>A Thankful Heart</u>

Two years ago, I had the incredible opportunity to visit Rome with two girlfriends for a weeks' holiday: months of checking last-minute flight websites every five minutes finally threw up some cheap tickets so we booked a hostel and off we went. Italy is one of my favourite places in the world, and I spent the whole week with a Cheshire-cat grin on my face, hardly able to believe that I was there. There was one day on the trip when we decided to visit one of the local beaches. After a bit of Googling, we got on a train, kept going past the beach that was packed with tourists, and managed to find the most beautiful beach, with just a few locals lazing around with their families. We spent the whole day sunbathing, reading, and snoozing in the sun – that day was like one giant exhale.

I decided to go for a dip in the afternoon; so I left my friends reading and swam out a bit, towards some rocks that went out into the sea from the coast. The water was unbelievably clear and blue as I looked out at the horizon; like a postcard picture. I began to walk out to the rocks and back, enjoying the feeling of my feet in the sand, and of pulling my legs through the water, trailing my hands over the gentle waves. It felt like God had landed me in this beautiful place, taken all the people and the busyness and the distractions away, and just given me some thinking space.

As I walked out, I set myself a challenge – I decided to think of something I was thankful for, for every step that I took. I was moving slowly enough that it was easy enough to get going. I managed to do this for the ten or fifteen minutes that it took me to reach the rocks – it felt like the easiest thing in the world.

The life that I had flown away from for the week wasn't this peaceful – it was the middle of quite a turbulent time, there were issues and questions and things to work out – but in the midst of that was a moment of beauty when I just focused on God. That holiday felt like a punctuation mark: I had flown away from one crazy season of my life, and flown back into new adventures, with a completely different perspective on the things that I was walking through. I had my eyes not on myself, my circumstances and my worries, but on God.

Thankfulness comes when we take our eyes off ourselves and our circumstances, and put them on God and all that He has done for us:

What is more, I consider everything a loss because of the surpassing worth of knowing Christ Jesus my Lord, for whose sake I have lost all things. I consider them garbage, that I may gain Christ and be found in him, not having a righteousness of my own that comes from the law, but that which is through faith in Christ – the righteousness from God on the basis of faith. (Philippians 3:8-9)

We can count all the things of this world – good and bad – rubbish, compared to knowing Christ Jesus. Living in this truth completely changes the way that we see life: instead of being ecstatic or devastated by the highs and lows of life, we get the constant joy of knowing Christ.

My prayer is that this book is something of a punctuation mark for you: A chance to leave some things behind, to fly away from some parts of your life. A chance to stop and take a moment to regroup with God, and then excitedly look forward to everything that He is going to do in and through you.

I Am Not a Millennial

When we live with our mind in heaven with our Father and our feet planted firmly on the ground in the world where He has put us, we live a life that is not deemed possible by the rest of our generation; a generation that has allowed our identity to be defined by the labels put on us. We are the Millennials, Generation Y; the by-products of protective parents in the age of terrorism and a media that focuses on the dangers in society; the generation that can expect to have difficulty finding a job; to not have enough money; to graduate university from into a bad economy, and to feel the consequences of the decisions of those that have come before. We're the generation that protests: politics, education costs, the legalisation of marijuana. We're the generation in which one in four of us have posted a video of themselves online, and the majority have multiple social media profiles and are carving out an online platform that will stay with us for our entire lives. Technology is ours, we're wired for it since birth, and the internet is all that we have ever known. We're the "thumb culture" generation, spending our lives on keyboards and mobiles and gaming controllers. We suffer from hyper-connectivity, trying to maintain anything up to 1500 connections, and we're experiencing all-time high levels of ADD.

For most of modern history, our society has fitted people into nice neat boxes, giving us generational identities that will define us in the history books. There were the Baby Boomers, the people characterised by a huge increase in birth rates following the second world war. Generation X followed them, and then Generation Y, the Millennials, each taking on their own identity. Generally, we're happy for our identity to be found in our generation, because that identity gives us a sense of belonging to something that is bigger than ourselves. Generally, it is assumed that members of the same generation will tend to hold similar beliefs, attitudes and behaviours, affecting their values, risk taking, social norms and the culture that they create. Generational identity gives us a way to bond with our peers – I'm with you; me too! We talk about generations in the same way that we talk about horoscopes; recognising that it is not the whole truth, but actively seeking out articles about our generation in order to find something to relate to. You only need to log on to Facebook to find something on your newsfeed: **You know you're a Millennial if…**

But, like any other stereotype, people do not fit into nice, neat boxes. While people are desperate for something to belong to and for ways connect with people, this is not the truth of who we are. The theories will tell you that historical events shape peer groups differently depending on the phase of life that they are in. We know that this is not the truth; there is real danger in doing things "the way that they are done", simply because that is the way that our generation has always done them. There is a danger in believing the things that we believe, simply because those are the things that our generation believes. There's a danger in treating people the way that we "should" treat them, simply because that is how our generation treats them.

It is possible to take a step back, and to look to God for the guidance than we need in our lives, rather than looking to the generational and cultural norms set by people around us. It is possible to know hope and truth in a world that tells us that there is no hope. It is possible to be united with others in a world that seeks to divide. It is possible to not see anyone as *less than*, but to know that we are all one in Christ Jesus.

So in Christ Jesus, you are all children of God through faith, for all of you who were baptised into Christ have clothed yourselves with Christ. There is neither Jew nor Gentile, neither slave nor free, nor is there male and female, for you are all one in Christ Jesus. (Galatians 3:26-28)

Christ did not come simply to change us individually; Christ came to save the world, and our identity is found not in being one with our generation, but in being one with all who belong to Christ. There is no class division, or gender division, nor racial division, for we are all one in Him. God has so much love for each of us as His sons and daughters that He does not make any of us inferior or less than anyone else – He is for us and does not put anything on us that is harmful. In a world where there was male domination, where the Jews were seen as closer to God, and where slaves were a part of society, Paul told each of us to serve one another and put others before ourselves. Unity fights against the enemy's plan to divide and bring darkness and hatred.

Our job is to be an **ambassador** of God's Kingdom; for our lives to point people towards the love of God, and to be vessels of grace, and peace, and truth. When people come into contact with me, my presence in their life should communicate that they are not "less than", they are not excluded, but that they are included in the love of Christ and they are accepted in the body of Christ. Instead of finding their identity in the rules that are set by a generation, they can find freedom in the love of Christ; they can find belonging in the body of Christ and know that they are part of a story that is much bigger than themselves.

> ***But whoever lives by the truth comes into the light, so that it may be seen plainly that what they have done has been done in the sight of God. (John 3:21)***

The dark is a comfortable place to be, because nobody can see you; it becomes really easy to put on a face, and live out an identity that is not our own. But we are called to come into the light, so that others might see that we do not live in our own strength, but in the strength that comes from God because of all that He has done. Christ has saved us, and we live by Him – let's live in a way that leaves no doubt of this. We are dead, and He lives in us; therefore, whatever we do is not us, but God – our lives are not about us, but a testimony to who God is and what He has done.

God has poured out His love into our hearts by the Holy Spirit, and when we give our lives as vessels to this love, He can pour out of us for all to see. Everything that God does is because of the love that He has for His people. Encounters with God's great grace bring hope; hope for a great life, for vision and for calling. I am a co-heir with God. I am the righteousness of God in Christ Jesus. I have a gospel that delivers me from death.

My hope in God delivers me from cynicism and the victim attitudes that can be found in our generation. Hope does not disappoint, because God has poured out His love into our hearts by the Holy Spirit. This unfailing love that is inside me means that I have hope in something that is much bigger than myself and the circumstances that I am in.

That's the question that comes up, time and time again, particularly when I'm working with young people – ***Heather, how are you always smiling? Why are you happy all the time?*** Joy is not about having a "fake it until you make it" attitude, and smiling when you don't feel like smiling because people might be convinced that you are happy; joy is about finding hope in the unfailing love that God has for you, and putting the truth of God over your perception of the world that you are in.

In a world that is cynical, hopeless, angry and bitter at the things that are happening to us, I am possible. In a generation that doesn't need a God because we can go after our own destiny, I am possible. In a generation that tells me that I should be lonely and that I need a boyfriend, I am possible. In a generation that does not look at the people that are struggling around us, but instead only focuses on our own happiness and achieving our own goals, I am possible. I will never be beaten down, and angry and bitter, because I have elected to sit in my identity as a child of God.

I AM A DREAMER: A POEM
ELAINE GRANT

i'm a dreamer, i am,

i'm made to see clearly,

made to see nearly as far as the horizon.

made for dancing on the ceiling,

banners streaming,

my eyes gleaming

with tears for that hope i see waiting;

but i won't wait,

no, i'll run straight.

straight down the road,

regardless of the load that i carry

i won't tarry,

i'll run wild and free,

'cause i'm a dreamer, you see.

i'm a dreamer, i am,

i'm made for glory.

this you see here is just part of my story,

but when i open my eyes

i can see blue skies dead ahead,

and i will tread

just that little bit lighter;

as i remember that i am a fighter

but this battle's already won

by the one who made the sun to rise.

and in his eyes

i see the prize

that i run for and towards:

and he says 'this is yours'.

i'm a dreamer, i am,

and not just for tomorrow;

but for today, i dare to believe.

TELL ME WHO I AM

i dare to have faith that sorrow can be replaced

that mourning can pass and joy take its place.

i dare to cry out that change is coming,

for i hear that rumbling,

thundering

sound of kingdom coming.

and the king himself is running here:

demons will flee, the dark will fear,

the prisoners walk free and the lost shout as they hear

the sound of belonging rising in the streets.

they stamp with their feet

to the beat of the free.

i am a dreamer,

a wild-eyed believer

in love that is neither

weak nor vague

but is specifically for me.

it screams from the page

as i read, my head reeling,

my heart slow to feel it;

my whole self reluctant to reach for it

in case

it crumbles,

and i stumble, left undone.

but as i stand paralysed,

i'm transfixed, and my eyes -

they're captivated.

i can't take it

but i also can't make it go away.

love reaches down, reaches in

to my heart; my soul begins

to shake / beat / sing

and i find myself grinning

like i've hit the winning inning

in the most beautiful game ever.

all my clever

words and rhymes just melt away

as love blazes.

TELL ME WHO I AM

i'm a dreamer, i am,

and it's not just me.

i believe / feel / see

that i'm part of a family

of dreamers:

reckless, beautiful, dancing believers.

i am not special,

any more than you.

i'm one of many, not just a few,

nor a few hundred, but thousands and thousands

together crying out and

remaking the future:

calling out to you that

i know a guy who has a dream.

and he's not dead, no.

he's wildly alive.

he speaks worlds into motion,

his vision makes life thrive.

he calls something out of nothing

and when he dreams he creates not streams

but rivers in the desert.

he is not <u>a</u> king but <u>the</u> king

and i dream because i know him;

who flung stars into space,

and when i see him face to face

my tiny plans are replaced

by his vision after vision,

dream after dream of grace.

i know who he is,

and i know who he made me:

i am made in his image,

i'm made to dream.

ABOUT THE AUTHOR

Heather is Basingstoke born and bred, and moved to Cambridge to study. She now lives and works in Cambridge as a youth worker, and has pioneered the I Am Project, a ministry with a heart for living outrageously and loving outrageously, knowing our identity is found in Christ.

She's a big coffee fan, and huge thanks go to Stir coffee shop in Cambridge, where most of this book was written.

Connect with us:

Visit www.facebook.com/iamprojectuk

Follow us on Instagram: @iamprojectuk

www.iamprojectuk.com

Made in the USA
Columbia, SC
21 November 2017